Enactments

EDITED BY RICHARD SCHECHNER

To perform is to imagine, represent, live and enact present circumstances, past events and future possibilities. Performance takes place across a very broad range of venues from city streets to the countryside, in theatres and in offices, on battlefields and in hospital operating rooms. The genres of performance are many, from the arts to the myriad performances of everyday life, from courtrooms to legislative chambers, from theatres to wars to circuses.

ENACTMENTS encompasses performance in as many of its aspects and realities as there are authors able to write about them.

ENACTMENTS includes active scholarship, readable thought and engaged analysis across the broad spectrum of performance studies.

singing emptiness

kumar gandharva performs the poetry of kabir

LINDA HESS

WITH CONTRIBUTIONS BY

U. R. ANANTHAMURTHY and ASHOK VAJPEYI

Seagull Books

LONDON NEW YORK CALCUTTA

Seagull Books, 2009

This edition, 2021

ISBN 978 0 8574 2 975 9

British Library Cataloguing-in-Publication Data

A catalogue record for this book is available from the British Library

Book designed by Sunandini Banerjee, Seagull Books, India

Printed and bound by WordsWorth India, New Delhi, India

CONTENTS

ON TRANSLITERATION

This book uses a modified scholarly transliteration in which certain letters are shown as they are pronounced rather than in the standard scholarly way, which would likely lead to mispronunciation. The exceptions to standard transliteration are the following: ś = sh; ṣ = sh; c = ch; ch = chh; ṛ = ṛi; jñ = gy. For mid-word nasal, 'n' or 'm' is used, whichever mostly closely approximates the right pronunciation; for end-word nasal, 'ṅ'. The Hindi letter representing the palatal 'd', and the same letter with a dot underneath in Hindi, are both transliterated as 'ḍ' (creating a slight ambiguity). For capitalized names of people and places, diacritical marks are not used.

PREFACE: THE STORY OF THIS BOOK

In 1991, the renowned Kannada writer U. R. Ananthamurthy visited the University of California, Berkeley, where I was then teaching. He was at that time head of the Sahitya Akademi, India's national academy of letters in Delhi. I had published a book a few years earlier on the fifteenth-century poet Kabir, which included many translations.

Sitting in a cafe on campus, drinking coffee, Ananthamurthy asked me if I knew the renditions of Kabir as sung by Kumar Gandharva. I didn't. Whatever he said next conveyed to me with lively energy that I ought to be listening to Kumar Gandharva. Then he made a suggestion: Collect all the Kabir poems sung by Kumar Gandharva and put them together in a little bilingual book, Hindi and English on facing pages. The Sahitya Akademi will publish it together with a cassette of Kumarji singing the bhajans (CDs were then unknown).

I agreed this would be a great project. And I did nothing about it. Ananthamurthy did not mention in our conversation that he had written a long poem about Kumar Gandharva and Kabir after a private concert he attended in Mysore in 1989. This would only come out when we met in Bangalore in 2004.

Soon after that first conversation, my friend Jeanne Fleming, an artist who lives on the Hudson River, north of New York City, sent me a tape. Her husband Harlan Matthews had been in India with his guru, Harish Jauhari, and they had attended a concert of Kumar Gandharva in Brindavan, organized by another guru called Shripadji. It was very hot, the end of summer. Everyone was eagerly waiting for the rain to start. After the concert, Shripadji called the singer to meet him privately. Only a few people were present, including Harlan and his guru. Shripadji asked the singer to sing a little more for him. 'You have given them the milk,' he is reported to have said jokingly, 'now give me the butter.' Kumar Gandharva and his wife and fellow singer, Vasundhara Komkali, then sang four more bhajans. Harlan happened to have a tape recorder. He pushed the button.

On the tape I heard Kumarji's voice singing Kabir for the first time. At that post-concert moment in Brindavan they had looked around for tablas but could only find one of the pair, the *bāyā*—the one played with the left hand. Someone was thumping simply on the *bāyā* as Kumarji and Vasundharaji began with '*Gurā to jī ne gyān kī jaḍiyā daī*'. The second song particularly haunted me in the days that followed: '*Ham pardesī panchhī bābā aṇī des rā nāhīṅ, oooh*' . . . 'I'm a bird from another country, *bābā*. I don't belong to this country.' The tune was simple, the rhythm slow, the refrain with its drawn-out, sliding three-note *oooh* at the end sang itself in my head over and over. Later, I found out that this melody was very close to its folk roots. While Kumarji had composed original melodies to many of the *nirguṇ* bhajans he sang, '*Ham pardesī panchhī bābā*' was sung almost identically to the style of the Malwa folksingers. In the middle of '*Ham pardesī panchhī*', a loud noise came up on the tape. Rain! The monsoon had broken just then. It was a downpour, getting louder as the song went on. At the end, Kumarji exclaimed, '*Vāh*! The rain has come!' The sound of pouring water continued through the next bhajan, '*Gurujī ne diyo amar nām*' (Guruji has given me a deathless name), and subsided in the last, '*Suntā hai guru gyānī*' (The guru, the wise one listens).

It took eight more years for me to reach Malwa, and even longer to arrive at the threshold of a project to explore oral and musical Kabir more deeply. In 2002, I began an association with Prahlad Singh Tipanya, a renowned Kabir folksinger whose village is about an hour's drive from Kumar Gandharva's home in Dewas. Through Prahladji's unstinting generosity, magnetic performances and flowing insights, I became drenched in Malwi folk Kabir. 'Oral Kabir' (which I had previously only talked and thought about) entered my body—words, melodies, rhythms, instruments, voices, all together.

Ashok Vajpeyi, eminent Hindi poet, essayist and cultural innovator, shared with me his powerful writings about Kumar Gandharva with whom he had had a close personal relationship. With unstinting generosity and wisdom, he advised and helped me from the beginning to the end of this project.

Ashok also introduced me to Kumar Gandharva's family, the Komkalis in Dewas—his wife Vasundhara, his daughter Kalapini and his grandson Bhuvanesh, all of whom are accomplished singers. They extended hospitality for which I will be forever grateful. They helped me with the texts of the songs, discussed the meanings of the words and recounted their memories and insights about Kumarji's way of singing *nirguṇ* bhajans. They showed me rare video footage of Kumarji, invited me for Guru Purnima, shared delicious food. Most of all, they let me listen to recordings of Kumar Gandharva's *nirguṇ* bhajans that were not available to the public. These listening sessions provided some of the most precious moments of my life.

In late 2007, the way was cleared for fulfilling the last part of the dream: creating a new CD to go with the book. Kalapini and Bhuvan worked with me to select and produce this beautiful set of five *nirguṇ* bhajans from live performances. Two of the songs have never been available to the public in any form, and the rest are new, longer versions of songs that have been available previously. For this, all lovers of Kumar and Kabir owe them deep gratitude.

Now, 18 years after Ananthamurthy originally proposed the idea, this book is coming out. A *sākhī* (couplet) of Kabir, frequently sung in Malwa, gives me some comfort as I contemplate this long time-span:

Dhīre dhīre re manā, dhīre sab kuchh hoy
mālī sīnche so ghaṛa, ritu āve phal hoy

Slowly, slowly, oh mind,
everything happens slowly.
The gardener pours hundreds of jars
of water
but fruit comes
only in season.

KUMAR GANDHARVA

A Poem by U. R. Ananthamurthy

Translated from Kannada by the author
and Linda Hess

I heard you first at Lalit Mahal[1]
with my daughter Anu,
thanks to Bhakre, that lover of Kalidasa.
By some amazing conjuncture
it was my birthday. I felt
I was being born again. I felt
the sound coming out of you
wave after wave
was there before you were born.[2]
I saw the listeners sitting before you
their boundaries
dissolved.

That shameless wanderer Kabir was riding on your back,[3]
reins completely loose, galloping
in ecstasy and yet contained
in melody and time.
Sometimes you'd stop
and comment in a high-pitched voice
as if to note your own location.
You were so pleased!
You swelled with pride
that such a vagabond would choose to ride
on your back for a while.
Singing, you laughed and smiled.

The song ended.
Bhakre gave you a Royal Salute.[4]
To let us know the ride was over,
you talked of trivial matters, casually.
With a gentleman's smile, you clinked your glass.
Your round *gandharva*[5] face
made you look like a grown-up child
but I was afraid to stand too close
to one who was touched by God.

You talked to me in Kannada.
Your intonations let me know
that you were from Belgaum. I even knew
your caste, from the words you chose.
Grumbling that your hand was swollen
with rheumatism, your leg too,
praising the Mysore climate,
praising my friend Ashok from Bhopal
a little too much, you showed you were
an ordinary fellow who could be

my friend. You conspired to free me
from the spell that held me.

Sky, birds, nature spirits,
rivers, jungles, hills, clouds,
raging cyclones, forest fires,
furtive ticklers, women whose eyes
brim with love, world-renouncers
who roar with laughter, goddesses
whose braids are made of night,
separated lovers blaming each other,
gods with dimpled chins,
shepherds playing flutes,
all this
had come cascading from your mouth.
To erase it, you asked
for garlic chutney, barley bread,
white radish, tender cabbage,
green coriander, fenugreek leaves,
chopped cucumber with lemon juice
and sprouted lentils.[6]
Thinking of your childhood,
like a tired trader coming home
from market, grumbling about the rheumatism
in your hands and legs,
as if you had nothing to do with Kabir,
you ate and drank happily.

I wondered how that mad Kabir
from the far north
could haunt our southern Kumar
of Belgaum.
I admired the celestial Gandharva's

worldly wisdom—how he freed himself
by hurling that mad creature
on innocents like us.

Ageing man
round cherubic face
swollen hand
gossiping and drinking
with humility and pride
half-asleep eyes
high-pitched voice
breathing
through just one lung[7]
balding head

I was astounded that God
became a tenant[8]
and prospered
in a place like that.

Notes

1 This poem was inspired by a private concert in Mysore in 1989.

2 *Nād*, translated as 'sound', suggests for the Indian reader a primordial sound associated with the moment of creation, the source of all sounds, and the fundamental vibration in music. It is also an important image in Kabir—in his poetry, *anahad nād*, the 'unstruck sound', is associated with moments of liberation. (See Introduction for more details.)

3 *Avadhūt*, hard to translate with the right flavour, has been rendered here as 'wanderer'. It is one of several words used for a person who

has renounced worldly life and wanders without possessions or attachments. Among the various types of renouncers, the *avadhūt* is likely to be more singular, solitary, mysterious, eccentric. Several of the *nirguṇ* bhajans that are translated in this book begin with an address to the *avadhūt*.

4 Royal Salute is the name of an Indian whiskey.

5 A beautiful semi-divine musician who plays in the heavenly courts of Hindu mythology.

6 The foods Kumar Gandharva relishes in his after-concert meal (especially the cucumber salad) are associated with the area around Belgaum in North Karnataka where he spent his childhood.

7 Kumar Gandharva was a child prodigy who developed into a unique musical genius. Originally named Shivputra Komkali, he was given the name Kumar Gandharva ('young celestial musician') in his youth, and it stuck for the rest of his life. In 1947, at 24, he was struck with tuberculosis. As there was no known cure, he was told he could never sing again. On doctors' advice, he moved from Bombay to Dewas, a hilly town in Madhya Pradesh that had clean air and a healthy climate. For nearly six years he was an invalid, largely bedridden and unable to sing. With the discovery of antibiotics, he recovered and resumed his singing career but, at that point, only one lung functioned. (See Introduction for more information on Kumarji's life.)

8 *Vokkalu*. Usually a landless farmer who takes up tenancy on someone else's land. Also used to refer to a devotee of Lord Venkateshvara. In both cases, a *vokkalu* is dependent—not his own person. In discussing this line with me, Ananthamurthy referred to the protagonist of Dostoyevsky's *The Idiot*. God can become a tenant in such a person: innocent, frail, naive, open. In such a tenancy, God thrives and prospers.

INTRODUCTION

Yā ghaṭ bhītar
IN THIS BODY[1]

You have just read (I hope) that wonderful poem by Ananthamurthy. Out of a night in Mysore in 1989, Ananthaji created a poem about Kumar Gandharva singing and eating, with a glimpse of conversation between the writer and the singer who both belonged to the Kannada country. In describing the music, he focused on Kumar's Kabir—and, we might say, on Kabir's Kumar. That shameless, wild Kabir rode on Kumar, and Kumar was so pleased!

It's hard to write without cliché or ponderous generalization about these two beings, K and K—one who was on the earth till recently, and the other, gone 500 years and so much harder to catch hold of, darting backwards like a phantom behind the flapping veils of myth and the pandits' expertise. Ananthamurthy has given us a fresh view of both.

Singing and eating: one boundless, erasing separations, opening a resonant space that exists beyond singer and listener; the other all earth, colour, taste, particularity.

It is common knowledge that the connection between Kabir and Kumar had to do with the first of these—singing in the *nirguṇ* mode, entering a space, a sound, a silence, something radically other than what we ordinarily know, beyond the mind's grasp, empty and still, vibrant and full. It is less common to realize that they also share an aliveness to the world, a presence in the body, without which their 'otherness' would perhaps fall down, powerless.

Many people who knew Kumarji tell stories of how he loved vegetables and flowers, birds, books and rain—how attentive he was to the things and the moments of this world. He enjoyed gardening and shopping; carried multiple shoulder-bags to the market so the fresh vegetables would not get crushed; engaged friends in long conversations about the beauties of *bhinḍī* (okra); set a tape recorder in the garden early in the morning to catch the conversation between two birds.

Shraddha Kirkire was a child when her parents, Channo and Neela, learned music from Kumarji and shared a close friendship with him. She tells of staying at the musician's house on holidays. Children liked to be around him: his quality of attention was such that they felt something was really going on, even when he wasn't doing much of anything. Shraddha remembers how he taught the children the fine points of watering plants. Once, for several consecutive days, he set his alarm for five in the morning and went out to record the voices of the *papihā* and the *koyal*.[2] Only at that moment could their voices be heard together (Virmani 2004a).

One day, in 2002, I visited the Komkali home in Dewas and found Vasundhara, his wife, stringing fragrant white jasmine. Their daughter Kalapini explained: every day my mother makes a string of these flowers for me to wear in my hair. We always remember how my father used to gather flowers from the garden in the morning, put a pile on the veranda and happily string garlands for the gods and gurus whose images were in the house.

One of Ashok Vajpeyi's prose-poems evokes Kumarji's rendition of Kabir's strange poem, '*Suntā hai guru gyānī*', in which a mysterious guru listens to a subtle voice in the sky. Though the imagery of the poem is quite unearthly, Vajpeyi locates the voice in the concrete details of Dewas at evening and Kumarji in his garden:

> *Gagan maṇḍal bīch meṅ āvāz* / In the middle of the sky circle a voice
>
> In the last light of evening, smoothing out the earth in the flowerbeds of his backyard. Mixing a little brown sugar with *nīm* petals, hands me a drink. He just read some prose of Vinda Karandikar—sated. Towel over his shoulder. His things, his flowers and plants wrapped in evening, drenched in the full maturity of artistic feeling.[3] Notes rising from his home and household, a voice in the circle of the sky, amazed and sad. Beneath the goddess's hill, sitting still amidst the emptiness and reverberation of his own voice[4] (1999: 19).

It is clear that what brought Kumar Gandharva and Kabir together must be explored in the realm of that key word, *nirguṇ*, indicating an ultimate reality that is beyond form, attribute, description. *Nirguṇ* will pull along with it some other key words, like *shūnya* (emptiness). There might be a temptation, when consorting with such words, to jump off the earth. But, as poets remind us, *shūnya* and *nirguṇ* are not far from where we are. They are to be found, if anywhere, amidst the colours of evening, the rough green symmetries of okra.

In another prose-poem, based on Kumarji's own statement, Vajpeyi catches exactly the point where the finite and the boundless coincide:

> *Gāte gāte roz martā hūṇ* / Every day I die singing
>
> He said, I'm a practitioner of the most perishable art: every day I die singing. That Kumar Gandharva who was singing, that raga Tilak Kamod he sang—both are dead. Tomorrow again Tilak Kamod will be sung, and Kumar Gandharva will sing, but not the same. In music whatever has happened once, by whatever person, may happen again, by that person again, but not the same (ibid.: 15).

On Guru Purnima[5] in July 2002, the Komkalis invited me to their home and showed some videos of Kumarji singing. At one point, he spoke before beginning a composition. Kalapini paraphrased his Marathi for me:

> Music does not mean repeating like a parrot. You don't learn something, then sing it the same way over and over. Each time I sing a *bandish*,[6] no matter how many times I have sung it before, for no matter how many years, it should be born anew in that moment. For example, I learned this *bandish* when I was eight. But it will be born now.

It is this presence in the ever-dying moment, this continuous readiness to die, and actual dying and being born each moment, that links Kumar Gandharva most completely to Kabir. Both lived with death; both went beyond fear. As Kabir often observes, a rare one understands this. A rare one understands the simultaneity of life and death, the impossibility of one without the other. But what does death mean? If Kumar Gandharva could die singing every day, it doesn't just mean the final departure of breath from the body.

Kabir is very insistent about making us face death. In poem after poem, he reminds us of how we're going to burn—our hair flaring up like dry grass, our bones igniting like sticks of wood. He has no shortage of metaphors for the body and its imminent disintegration. It's a house whose walls are made of sand; a musical instrument whose strings snap and whose soundbox cracks when the player goes away. It's a ball of paper that melts in the rain. It's a glass bangle; a drop of dew.

But there is something interesting about Kabir's treatment of the body: it is not just a throwaway, a worthless thing. Yes, our pride in the body, our attachment to its appearance and our clinging to the delusion that it will last forever are radically misplaced. Yet there are, perhaps, as many songs referring to the wonder and splendour within the body as there are insisting on its mortality and disposability.

> Who can know this? The one who knows!
> Without a teacher, the world is blind.

In this body forests and hamlets, right here mountains and trees
In this body gardens and groves, right here the one who waters them
. . .[7]

In this body seven oceans, right here rivers and streams
In this body moon and sun, right here a million stars

In this body lightning flashing, right here brilliance bursting
In this body the unstruck sound roaring, streams of nectar pouring

In this body the three worlds, right here the one who made them
Kabir says, listen seekers: right here my own teacher.[8]

In countless Kabir songs heard in the countryside around Dewas, the body, figured as a *ghaṭ* or clay pot, is shown to contain the all-illuminating light, the unstruck sound that reverberates through the universe. The body is at once the precious place of presence and the instantly perishable pot that crumbles into dust. Kumar Gandharva and Kabir remind us of both these realities. A folk bhajan popular in Malwa concludes:

Mātī kā sab bāman baniyā, mātī kā sakal pasārā
In mātī meṅ sab koī milanā, kah gaye sāhib kabīrā

The priest is dust, the shopkeeper is dust,
the whole creation is dust.
In this dust, we all meet.
Kabir keeps telling you this!

Kabir also keeps telling us not to miss what's going on:

Vaṭhe gayoṛa phir nahīṅ āyo, aisā avsar kar re

What's gone will not come back,
so live this moment now.[9]

TWO SUBJECTS

So far I have been talking as if I were engaged in a conversation with people who already know Kumar Gandharva and Kabir. But for readers who have not yet made their acquaintance, let me briefly introduce the two figures whose relationship is the subject of this book.

Kabir was a poet of the fifteenth century who lived in Varanasi, in the present state of Uttar Pradesh. Stories about his life come to us as legends, most of them unverifiable. But everyone agrees that he grew up in a family of Muslim weavers and that he practised the weaving craft himself. Most scholars believe that Kabir was unlettered and composed all his works orally. His poems were preserved first orally, then in manuscripts and books. Their most vibrant life is in the form of songs. They are sung now, as they have been for over five centuries, in many musical styles and with the flavours of many dialects of Hindi. Because Kabir did not write, and because oral traditions are so fluid and open, it is virtually impossible to identify any particular compositions as definitely his. Discussions about textual histories and 'authenticity' may be sought elsewhere.[10] In this book, we will partake freely of the oral tradition, accepting as Kabir's *bāṇī* (verbal expressions) whatever Kumarji and the folksingers of Malwa have sung.

Kabir's compositions have a uniquely powerful style, expressing his own spiritual awakening, urging others to wake up and criticizing delusion in individuals and society. His voice is fearless, direct, iconoclastic and anti-authoritarian. The poetry has a vivid streak of social criticism, making trenchant observations on caste prejudice, religious sectarianism, hypocrisy, arrogance and violence. At the same time, it is profoundly inward-looking. It examines the nature of mind and body, points out the tangle of delusions in which we live, urges us to wake up and cultivate consciousness. The imminence of death and the transience of all things are frequently invoked. The journey within is permeated with the imagery of yoga—its map of a subtle body made of energy, lotus-centres, coursing breath-streams, sound and light. A key word associated with Kabir's spiritual stance is *nirguṇ*, indicating an ultimate reality that cannot be visualized in form or described in language. While invoked negatively, it conveys, simultaneously, emptiness and fullness.

Kumar Gandharva was born in 1924 as Shivputra Siddharamaiya Komkali, the son of a musical family in Belgaum District of northern Karnataka. He showed signs of musical genius by age five, sang solo on stage at 10, and was soon christened Kumar Gandharva—a name that stuck for the rest of his life. When he was 11, his father sent him to Bombay to study with master B. R. Deodhar; he was, according to one writer, 'as well known as his teacher' at that point (Menon 2001: 51). He quickly mastered the knowledge and technical skills that were placed before him and was teaching at the school before he was 20.

By the 1940s, Kumar Gandharva was a 'prince of music', a star performer praised by critics in the highest terms (Virmani 2004b). In 1947, he married Bhanumati, a student of vocal music at Deodhar's school. That same year, he was diagnosed with a virulent case of tuberculosis and told that he could never sing again. Soon, he moved with Bhanumati to Dewas, a town in western Madhya Pradesh known for its goddess temple on a hill and its healthy climate. He was only 24.

There ensued six years of illness and silence. Doctors told him that if he tried to sing, it would kill him. There was little hope of recovery. Six years of silence for any singer would be a trial beyond imagining, but for him who was born to sing, whose genius revealed itself when he was five, who at 18 was restlessly seeking a way to go beyond the mastery that he already possessed, it was a supreme test of the will to live. Well-known stories of this period narrate how he lay in bed and listened to the sounds around him—birdsong, wandering street-singers, the wind. A man who took care of him told Raghava Menon that he hummed almost inaudibly through those years:

> Krishnan Nambiar . . . looked after and managed the Kumar household in all those years that Kumar lay in bed debarred from singing. . . . When I asked Nambiar [on a visit in the 1950s] whether Kumar sang at all during his illness, he replied that he did not think so, but there was this one thing. He seemed constantly to be humming something to himself, so softly that you did not hear anything unless you went close to him (Menon 2001: 72–3).

Such intimacy with silence, such a long letting go and waiting, letting go of everything, and listening—this surely prepared the ground from which *nirguṇ* would later blossom in Kumarji.

In 1952, streptomycin became available. Kumarji took it, recovered and began to sing again. One of his lungs was destroyed. He sang with the other for the rest of his life—for 40 more years.

The shocks and bereavements were not over. His wife Bhanumati, who had nursed him and given him courage throughout his illness, died giving birth to their second son in 1961.

Later, Kumarji married Vasundhara; she became his singing partner as well as his partner in life. Vasundhara is still a vibrant performer who has received many honours. Their daughter Kalapini carries on the tradition, performing widely in India and beyond. Kumarji's grandson Bhuvanesh has begun a promising career as a singer.[11] The first son of Kumarji and Bhanumati, Mukul, is also a highly reputed singer.

As a Hindustani classical singer, Kumar Gandharva was influential and unconventional. He was adored and revered by many, dismissed by some. He experimented dangerously with established ragas and created new ones that have since been accepted in the canon. He had a lively, questioning intellect and an insatiable curiosity. He was formidably independent and did not identify himself with any gharana.[12]

Sunil Mukhi, who created the first wide-ranging website on Kumar Gandharva, has summed up the artist's unique qualities thus:

> Kumarji's strongest point, in my opinion, was an ability to place his own distinctive interpretation on anything that he sang, and a very wide repertoire that included standard raagas, rare and complicated raagas, raagas that he invented (or, as he preferred to say, 'discovered'), folk songs, particularly from the Malwa region of Madhya Pradesh, *bhajans* (whose status as a form of classical music was greatly elevated by his contributions) and Marathi stage songs ('natya-sangeet').[13]

Two of these points are especially relevant to Kumarji's relation to Kabir: first, that he became deeply interested in Malwi folk music, which he listened to, performed and used creatively in his compositions; second, that he brought *bhajans*—devotional songs whose words were composed by the great Bhakti poets of the fourteenth–sixteenth centuries in Hindi and Marathi—to the classical stage in an unprecedented and lasting way.

Kumarji sang *saguṇ* as well as *nirguṇ* bhajans—*saguṇ* referring to a supreme being who is describable in terms of forms, attributes and narratives. He sang the poetry of Mirabai, Surdas, Tulsidas, those lovers of Krishna and Rama, the Vaishnav avatars whose lore is full of stories and descriptions. But the list of well-known *saguṇ* bhajans is much shorter. Kumarji's songs of Kabir and Gorakhnath acquired a fame of their own. He had a special affinity with *nirguṇ*.

WORDS WITHOUT EDGES[14]

Kumarji's Nirguṇ *Collection*

Today it is only a 15-minute walk from a neighbourhood of houses and shops near the heart of Dewas to the quiet portal of the Shilnāth Dhūnī Sansthān, where Nath yogis used to gather around a fire that was first built by Shilnath, a great yogi who settled there in 1901. Still the last half-mile out of the commercial centre is peaceful, amidst trees, open fields, the sound of birds. In Shilnath's time, it must have felt much farther from town. There is a gateway building, tall and thin, its four storeys marked with windows and wrought-iron grilles, its walls so mottled with a mossy overlay that you can hardly see the pink colour underneath. Beyond this arched entryway is an open space, then another arch in a building whose pleasantly peeling brick-red surfaces seem to blend in with the surrounding trees, flowers and earth.

This Sansthān, or institution, was created to honour and memorialize the yogi who blessed the area by living here for nearly 20 years. Shilnath's *dhūnī*—the fire that signifies a sadhu's essential homelessness and his *tapasyā* (ascetic and meditative practice believed to generate heat, *tapas*)—has been kept burning since his departure from Dewas in 1920. The fire is now protected by a roof and surrounded by several buildings. One of these structures was built in Shilnath's lifetime. Fortunate visitors may be ushered upstairs to the room where he stayed. A trap-door in the floor opens to a small cave-like chamber where he meditated. For many years, the Shilnath *dhūnī* was a place where Nath sadhus and lay devotees gathered and sang *nirguṇ* bhajans bearing the signature lines of Kabir, the Nath Panth's founder Gorakhnath and a few other poets. Kumar Gandharva used to go there often.

When I first visited the Sansthān in 2002, the fire burned in the midst of a tree-dotted open space. Arriving in 2006, I was greeted by a huge expanse of grey cement about five feet off the ground. The circular fireplace was like a little island in this vast cement sea. Many half-finished concrete pillars reached skyward, iron rods protruding from their tops, tattered orange flags fluttering from the rods. The devotees of Shilnath were building an impressive temple for him.

I turned toward the oldest building, where Shilnath himself used to stay. The facade has Hindi couplets painted on it, most of them by Kabir. The ground floor is a large hall, its tiles and flagstones uneven and cracking in pretty patterns. Many likenesses of the seated Shilnath—an imposing, thin man, unclothed except for a loincloth, with beard and long matted hair, leaning slightly forward over his crossed legs—adorn the area. The visitor is drawn to the far left corner where a recessed shrine, its dominant colour an intense red, contains relics from Shilnath's time: wooden sandals, a broad seat covered in gold-trimmed maroon cloth, two long mirrors flanking the seat. Both mirrors have embossed writing on them; the one on the left has a Kabir poem: '*Uḍ jāegā hans akelā, jag darshan kā melā*' (It will fly away alone, the swan / What a sight: the carnival of this world!). Kumar Gandharva discovered the mirror-text here and set it to an exquisitely beautiful melody.[15] It was in this hall, or outside by the *dhūnī* when there were trees instead of a cement slab, that Kumar Gandharva sat with others who had been attracted by Shilnath's fire, conversing, listening and singing. It is also at the Shilnath *dhūnī* that he would hear both sadhus and householders singing.

The Nath yogis—also called *kānphaṭas*, 'split ears' or 'pierced-ears' because of the large earrings that they put on at the time of initiation [see White (1996) and Briggs (1973)]—are an old sect founded by the quasi-legendary Gorakhnath, whose shadowy existence has been placed at various times from the ninth to the twelfth century. Often wandering alone, they are the likely prototype for the *avadhūt* addressed in many Kabir poems, including three sung by Kumarji. Naths practice yogic postures, *prāṇāyama* (breathing exercises) and meditation. The yogic map of the body, with its subtle energy channels and series of *chakras* or lotus-like energy-centres starting at the base of the spine and ending with the thousand-petalled lotus at the crown of the head, is basic to their teachings and songs. References to this vision of the body and to yogic practices of centring the breath and reversing the normal downward flow of energy (*prāṇa*) occur frequently in Kabir as well.[16] The culmination of yogic experience is characterized by sound and light, with an emphasis on sound. It is touched off at a certain place in the body: the *gagan manḍal*, the circle or dome of the sky. The 'sky' is in the dome of the skull, and it is also in the infinite space above. Body and cosmos completely resonate with each other in this experience.

Shilnath decided to leave Dewas in 1920, to spend his last days at Haridwar in the foothills of the Himalayas. Within a year of reaching Haridwar, he knew his end was near. He asked his disciples to dig a pit.[17] Then he asked one of them to sing Kabir's '*Ham pardesī panchhī bābā, aṇī des rā nāhīṅ*'. Sitting in a meditative posture, listening to this song, he expired.[18] Some 70 years later, Nath Panthis of Dewas burst into song at Kumar Gandharva's funeral. The song they sang was '*Ham pardesī panchhī bābā*'.[19]

In 1976, Ashok Vajpeyi, Rameshchandra Shah, Rahul Barpute and Mangalesh Dabral engaged Kumar Gandharva in a five-hour interview, which was published in Vajpeyi's *Bahurī Akelā: Kumār Gandharva par Kavitāen aur Nibandh* [Among Many, Alone: Poems and Essays on Kumar Gandharva, 1999)].[20] One question concerned the sources of his Kabir texts and his process of selection:

> From a number of *bhakti* poets you have made an astonishing (*adbhūt*) selection that has not only musical but also literary importance. Especially your Kabir songs—most of them are not to be found in the available collections. So this is also a new exploration of Kabir.

> From what point of view do you choose or search for the compositions that you will sing? (ibid.: 91)

In answering this question, Kumarji refers first to an obscure book of *sant bāṇī* (*nirguṇ bhajan* texts) that came his way:

> There are books of *sant vāṇī* that don't reach most people, but do reach Kumar Gandharva. . . . Many books get published but aren't seen by anybody, right? Out of affection, when people come across a certain book, they give it to Kumar. At some point in history someone published it, and then it disappeared. The Nath sect used to be very prominent in Dewas. In the time of Shilnath Maharaj [misspelled in the book as Shrinath], many great Nath *sādhūs* used to come here. They were all singers in the oral tradition. *Kānphaṭas.* Shilnath Maharaj published those songs. You also find Gorakh and Machhinder there.[21] A devotee came and gave me the book (ibid.: 91).

This book, *Shrī Shīlnath Śhabdāmṛit*, was originally published in 1915—during Shilnath's lifetime. I have a photocopy of the second edition, printed in 1923.[22] A note at the beginning mentions that, although the bhajans should have been checked for accuracy, there was no one qualified to do this. So it has been printed just as it was, in response to requests from Shilnath's devotees.

Of the 30 *nirguṇ* bhajans collected in this book, 21 are included in *Shrī Shīlnāth Śhabdāmṛit.*[23] One more, though not in the book, was found by Kumarji on the mirror in the Shilnath shrine. The *Śhabdāmṛit* contains 500 bhajans, of which the overwhelming majority bear Kabir's signature line. One might expect to find more songs of Gorakhnath and other Nath poets in such a collection; the predominance of Kabir speaks to the esteem in which he was held by Nath yogis, at least in the last century or two. The proportion of Kabir to others in this selection of Kumarji's *nirguṇ* bhajans—21 attributed to Kabir, five to Gorakhnath, one to Shivguru, one to Devanath, two with no signature line—roughly reflects the proportions of Kabir, Gorakhnath and others in the *Śhabdāmṛit.*

So the source of Kumarji's *nirguṇ* texts, which are not to be found in standard publications, becomes fairly clear: mainly the Shilnath *dhūnī* and Shilnath's own printed collection. Still, there were 500 bhajans in the *Śhabdāmṛit*, and he sang only about 30. Some principles of selection were clearly at work.

In the interview, after mentioning Shilnath's collection, Kumarji speaks of a deeper process, more like a recognition than a choice:

> When you want to create a beautiful form, choosing isn't easy. Sometimes, on a certain day, it says—this is what I am. When I want to compose a bhajan, I don't just read the poetry. I look, then I leave it alone, look and leave it alone. I try to understand the field of feeling. What does it want to say? What was this poet's situation? If I had been the author, how would I have said it? The whole thing that he has said, I say it myself—then I think, no, that's not it. There must be something higher that can be said through the medium of *svara*. Only then is there some point [in composing].
>
> The choice of some poems also depends on the tempo. At a certain moment it comes before me as a song . . . how the vowels and consonants fall, what it is saying, and how what it says come forth through the tempo. To sing a bhajan with a good voice is one thing, but to really express it is something completely different. There's one *bhajan*, '*Māyā mahāṭhaganī ham jānī*' [Maya's the great swindler—now I know], and a similar one, '*Ramaiyā kī dulhin lūṭā bāzār*' [Ram's bride has looted the market]. Both of these bhajans by Kabir express the same idea, but the meters are different. I took up '*Māyā mahāṭhaganī*'. From a musical point of view, what is being said comes across better in that one. A couple of years passed, and it was still sitting there. It didn't click. After about two-and-a-half years, it took shape. It was beautiful[24] (Vajpeyi 1999: 92).

Kumarji emphasizes that it is not meaningful to choose a text for musical composition unless there is something in the text that can be expressed only through *svara*. We will soon consider more fully the meaning of *svara*. Here I will suggest that his invocation of it in this statement points to the *nirguṇ* quality of the text.

In an interview with Shabnam Virmani (2004c), Krishna Nath, a writer and friend of Kumar Gandharva, gave further glimpses of Kumarji's search for the *nirguṇ* quality of music and his process of composing Kabir bhajans.

> I put this question to Kumar Gandharva when he came on his last trip to Banaras . . . I asked him: 'Your music—where does it come from? Is it only in the *svaras*, or does it arise from the space beyond the *svaras*?' That evening he didn't respond. Next day at breakfast he asked me, 'How did you come up with that question? That is a question I have been asking myself for the last forty years. Where does my music come from? Does it come only from the notes, tempo, rhythm (*sur, lay, tāl*)? Is it bound within the seven notes of the scale (*saptam svaroṅ meṅ hī bāndhā huā hai*)? Or is it from a place where these things don't reach, from where some hint (*sanket*) arises, some suggestion (*dhvani*) of sound or resonance (*nād-ninād*). Is this where music lies? To this day, I can't decide. Certainly it is not bound within the notes. Sometimes I try to catch hold of it, but it can't be grasped, it keeps receding farther and farther away from me.'
>
> Then since he was one of the foremost singers of Kabir of the age, I asked him, 'Why did you bind Kabir into *rāgas*?' He said, 'No, no, I didn't do anything, this exists in Kabir's poem itself. These *rāgas*, I have not imposed them from elsewhere. If you listen closely they lie embedded in Kabir's poem itself. All I have done is to open them up and sing them for you. There is nothing here that is mine.' This was his humility and modesty at one level, but there is also truth in it.[25]

Thematically, many of the texts Kumarji chose were the most *nirguṇ* of the *nirguṇ*. He did not use any of the Kabir songs that feature social commentary or satire, though such songs are available in the *Śhabdāmṛit*. His bhajans emphasize yogic experience, death and transiency, sleep and awakening, the guru's gracious gift of transformation. Many of them play at the edge of language. They sing of emptiness (*shūnya*), a space that is utterly different (*nyārā*), something that is subtle (*jhīnī*), almost beyond imagining.

Sakhiyā vā ghar sab se nyārā

OH MY FRIEND, THAT HOUSE IS UTTERLY DIFFERENT

On an old tape of a 1980 *nirguṇ* bhajan concert, I heard Kumarji getting ready to enter into '*Māyā mahāṭhaganī ham jānī* '. For me, who had never heard him live, it was a rare opportunity to hear a different rendition of a song that was familiar in its published version. It also opened the space of his actual singing in a way that the economics of studio recordings do not permit. With a sense of privilege and sweet intimacy, I heard him begin in a quiet and leisurely way, as if there were no one listening: . . . *sā . . . <nī . . . <nī sā . . . <nī sā . . . <nī sā . . . ga sā . . . ga sā . . . <nī sā . . . <nī . . . sā <nī . . . sā ga sā . . . ga sā . . . <nī sā . . . <nī sā pa ma ga pa ma ga re sā . . . ga re sā . . . ga re sā . . . ga re sā . . . <nī . . . sā . . . <nī sā . . . ga sā . . . ga sā <nī sā . . . re . . . sā <nī . . . sā re ni . . . ga . . . ga pa ma ga re sā . . . pa . . . pa . . . pa ma ga re sā . . . ga re sā . . . <nī sā . . . sā ga pa ma . . . ga re sā.*

From there he slid into *ṭhaganī ham jānī*, like someone slipping down a smooth bank into a quiet river.

It occurred to me to use three key words—*nyārā, jhīnī, shūnya*—like notes or *svaras*, as a way to explore major themes of *nirguṇ* Kabir/Kumar.

Nyārā calls to us as much through the two great open *ah* sounds as through the meaning. The meaning is 'different' or 'other'. Utterly other. Not just different, but different from anything we can conceive of. Kumarji sang three Kabir *bhajans* where the key word, repeated over and over in the refrain, is *nyārā*: '*Sakhīyā vā ghar sab se nyārā*'; '*Rām niranjan nyārā re*' (Unstained Ram is utterly other); and '*Avadhūtā kudrat kī gat nyārī*' (Oh solitary wanderer, nature's ways are strange).

Nyārā also comes up in one of the stanzas of '*Ham pardesī panchchī bābā*':

> *Chhāyā baiṭhūṅ agnī vyāpe, dhūp adhik sitalāī*
> *Chhāyā dhūp se satguru nyārā, maiṅ satguru ke māī*
>
> Sitting in shadow, I'm on fire.
> In sunlight, I'm cool.
> My true guru is beyond

sun and shade.
I dwell in the guru.

In '*Rām niranjan*', Kumarji lingers at the beginning on the short refrain: *Rām niranjan nyārā re, anjan sakal pasārā re* (Unstained Ram is utterly other. This spreading world is eye-shadow, brother). He keeps repeating, altering the phrasing, entering, warming up, exploring, letting his voice open to an 'ahh' that runs upward and downward. *Nyārā* is the ruling word of this *bhajan*, in both sound and meaning. It is a wide open word, defined by its two 'ah' vowels. He sings *nyārā* again and again, opening his voice to the sky. The repetitions return between stanzas and at the end, filling the song with this open feeling. Then, the echo of *niranjan* and *anjan* and the pleasing rhyme of *nyārā* and *pasārā* create a melodious beauty in the ear and shifting realities in the mind that are very difficult to translate on a page.

Unstained Ram is utterly other.
This spreading world is eye-shadow, brother.
Eye-shadow creation, the sound of Om,
eye-shadow vast expanse of space,
eye-shadow Brahma, Shiva, Indra,
eye-shadow Krishna with all his girlfriends.

Eye-shadow poetry, eye-shadow Veda,
eye-shadow all your fine distinctions,
eye-shadow science, story, recitation,
eye-shadow all your useless information. . . .

Nyārā is contrasted, but also continuously rhymed, with *pasārā*—literally, 'something spread out', thus all existence, the vast expanse of creation. Similarly *niranjan*—stainless or without mark—is contrasted and rhymed with *anjan*—a black mark or, in everyday usage, black eye-shadow. *Niranjan* and *nyārā* seem to represent the unlimited, *anjan* and *pasārā* the limited. The poet lists various elements of creation, from the commonplace to the subtle and lofty, repeatedly declaring that these are not *it*, that the truth is something else, *nyārā*. It is tempting to think that he thus devalues and dismisses this world and our embodied life. Such a conclusion seems too simpleminded to me. Kumar and Kabir direct our attention to a borderline where language, with its dualistic imperatives, is not sufficient.

Kabir plays with language, with two-and-one:

> If I say one, it isn't so.
> If I say two, it's slander.
> As it is, so it is,
> Kabir says
> thoughtfully.[26]

A common formula in the poetry is *akath kathā* or *akath kahānī* (as in '*Māyā mahāṭhaganī ham jānī*' and '*Naiyā morī nīke chālan lāgī*' (My little boat is sailing smoothly). It means 'untellable story', or, more literally (since the two words have the same root), 'unutterable utterance'. But Kabir keeps saying things, despite his protestation that the most important thing is unsayable. In Malwi folk Kabir I often hear the word *sen*—a sign, a hint.[27] A guru may give a subtle, indirect, possibly playful indication. Mostly we miss it. In '*Sakhiyā vā ghar sab se nyārā*', he concludes enigmatically:

> Where that one lives,
> there's nothing.
> Kabir says, I've got it!
> If you catch my hint, you'll find
> the same place—
> no place.

The word *jhīnī*, 'subtle', also hints at an understanding to which Kabir's poetry and Kumarji's music may bring us. The most famous of all Kabir songs, '*Jhīnī jhīnī bīnī chadariyā*' (Subtle, subtle, subtle, / is the weave / of that cloth), describes the body as a piece of cloth. This cloth is subtle. If we scrutinize the fine weave, we will see shining passageways with energy running up and down, we will see lotuses blooming and breathing. *Jhīnī* is also the nature of a voice that the poet and singer hear, resonating in a sky that is both inner and outer. We will speak more of that voice in the next section.

What to say of *shūnya*, a word that means zero, a Buddhist and yogic term usually rendered in English as 'empty'?

Perhaps the most enigmatic bhajan that Kumarji sang is '*Shūnya gaḍh shahar*' [In the empty fort, a city]. According to a 2006 newspaper column, it was the last *nirguṇ* bhajan that he composed.[28] The refrain, while difficult to understand, is strangely compelling in imagery and melody:

Shūnya gaḍh shahar shahar ghar bastī, kaun sūtā kaun jāge hai
Lāl hamāre ham lālan ke, tan sūtā brahm jāge re

In the empty fort, a city
In the city, a settlement.
Who sleeps? Who wakes?
My love is mine, I am my love's.
The body sleeps, the spirit wakes.
In the empty fort, a city
In the city, a settlement.[29]

I found '*Shūnya gaḍh shahar*' almost impossible to translate. Finally, I gave up. Then it became easier. The text is not logical. It does not cohere. Mysterious expressions remain unexplained. Connections are unclear. But when Kumar Gandharva sings, there seems to be no problem.

The word *shūnya* rules. It changes everything it touches. The poet and the singer take us inside this fort city that has its own light and shadow. Anything can happen here. There's a dreamlike feeling to the song. The focus can change at any instant. We see a lotus, get a closeup of its central petals, a bee buzzing over it. Then we're looking at a city with 10 gates, a lone yogi forever circumambulating it. There are metaphors for body and mind, something being ground up and served in a drink. A firepit, a practitioner in the fire. Five disciples muttering 'Unseen'. Three heavenly women, a son born of a virgin, happy parents. Then suddenly it ends, with Gorakh declaring that he meditates on one, indivisible.[30]

The text raises questions, the song dissolves them. *Shūnya gaḍh shahar*, the voice repeats, moving down in the register, taking us beneath the surface, leading with *shūnya*. *Shahar ghar bastī*, with an empty beat before *bastī*, then an almost flat, spoken repetition of *bastī*, just to assure us that he means it, a *bastī*, a settlement in the midst of emptiness. A quick movement between a seemingly metaphysical question—who sleeps? who wakes?—and a nonsequitur declaration—my love is mine, I am my love's. An answer to the question—body sleeps, spirit wakes. The movement of the voice on the final *re* takes us in, around, down, in a minor key, down to a deeper level in this surreal fort.[31] We are ready for anything, as long as this voice keeps leading us.

Near the end of another bhajan, '*Nirbhay nirguṇ guṇ re gāūngā*' (Fearless, formless, / that's the form I'll sing, yes), we come to the climax of a yogi's process of inner unification:

Shūnya shikhar par anahad bāje, rāg chhattīs sunāūngā

On the peak
of emptiness,
where the unstruck sound
resounds, I'll sing
thirty-six ragas.

Shūnya is a place to listen and a place to sing. Singing and listening—the same place.[32]

Suntā hai guru gyānī

THE GURU, THE WISE ONE, LISTENS

Kabir signs off nearly every poem with an exhortation to listen, addressed in a familiar and informal way to whoever might hear his song: '*Kahe kabīr suno bhāī sādho*'—'Kabir says, listen, brother, seeker.' On a superficial level, he's just signing off, as is conventional in Bhakti poetry. But his choice of verb—'listen'—is unconventional; in fact, its constant use is unique to Kabir in North Indian Bhakti literature.

Can we link this unusual signature line to the imagery with which he consistently expresses his deepest spiritual experience? It makes sense, though the connection has not been discussed in scholarly works that I have read. Kabir continually refers to ultimate reality and transformative experience in terms of sound. He suggests this sound through words like *shabda, nām, nād, anahad nād*—word, name, sound, unstruck sound. Poetically, the sound may be figured as instrumental music, a bell, a singing voice, thunder.

The notion of sound as ultimate reality—called *nāda brahmaṇ*—goes far back in Indian philosophy. Some would point to it first in the Om of the *Upanishads*; some would reach earlier, to the sung mantras of the *Sāma Veda*. Its elaboration comes later, associated with the practice of yoga, where one works with breath and energy in one's own body. Sanskrit musical treatises describe music as yoga and speak of the musician's quest in terms of realizing *nāda brahmaṇ*.[33] Kabir was steeped in the lore of the Nath Yogis who described the consummation of yogic practice in terms of a sound that resonates within and beyond the body.

One of Kumarji's most famous Kabir *bhajans* is built around the image of someone who listens:

> *Suntā hai guru gyānī, gagan meṅ āvāz ho rahī jhīnī jhīnī*
>
> The guru, the wise one
> listens. A voice vibrates
> in the sky, subtle,
> very subtle.

Kumarji tells the story of how he heard this song from a wandering yogi. In the process, he comments on the special way of singing *nirguṇ*:

> The way of singing *nirguṇī bhajans*—it is something unique. Especially those people who belong to the Nath sect, who have very little to do with settled habitations—their world is completely different. Their life is different, their ways are different. Forget the ones who just wander [singing] to fill their stomachs. But the real ones—the ones who really have faith in this kind of life—the voice that comes out of them—that's what I try to practice. One day I was sitting on the veranda of the bungalow where I used to live. A man came to beg. He was singing '*Suntā hai guru gyānī*' . . . . They usually sing until they get some money. It's not that he was singing very well. But I thought: this is the *nirguṇī* voice; I should definitely prac-

tice this. The next day I composed '*Suntā hai guru gyānī*'. The quality of creating emptiness (*shūnya*) in *nirguṇ* is amazing. It comes from that carefree, nonattached state. Throw—but it shouldn't hurt. Throw anything at all, even a very sharp thing, but it shouldn't hurt. A person should just enjoy it: hey, man, he threw that one well, didn't he? In *nirguṇ*, this way of expressing, of throwing the voice, is a natural part of their lives. Without having that kind of nature, you can't put forth that kind of voice. Their voice matches their mind. *Maiṅ jagūṅ mhārā satguru jāge, ālam sārā sovai* . . . 'I am awake, my true guru is awake, the whole universe is sleeping'—that is their world. When they sing, at that moment, who is there? No one is there. The *svaras* that come out there are not the *svaras* that come out in the drawing room, are they? *Nirguṇ* should convey a sense of aloneness (1976 interview by Vajpeyi et al., in Vajpeyi 1999: 91–2).

Among several noteworthy points in this remarkable passage is Kumarji's appreciation of and determination to learn from the humble beggar who passed by and sang a fragment of a song in a not-very-good voice. Kumarji understood that the beggar had something he did not. Though many who knew him described Kumar Gandharva as conveying an unusual sense of inner detachment, he still lived in a bungalow with his family and possessions, with his garden to cultivate. He was a man accustomed to drawing rooms. The wandering singer had a freedom and openness that belong to those who have no houses and don't care who they impress; who are accustomed to wandering alone, only occasionally recognizing a kindred spirit.

Neela Kirkire spoke of her own experience of hearing Kumar Gandharva sing *nirguṇ*:

Nirguṇ and *saguṇ* are two streams among the *sants*. In *saguṇ* there are Ram and Krishna, there are objects of devotion. . . . *Nirguṇ* is related to nature (*nisarg*). There is no concrete image to worship. The sky, the sun and moon and so on, are inside the body. The *sants* speak of channels in the body, *inglā, pinglā, sushumnā*, left, right, and center, which are also called by the names of rivers, Ganga, Yamuna, Saraswati. This is nature—it is what gives us life. These Kabir Panthis sing for their own pleasure.[34] When they sing under the open sky

> for their own joy, their existence, the spirit (*ātmā*) that is within them enters the boundless (*nirākār*). That is called *nirguṇ*. What they express was in Kumar Sahib. That total carefree abandon[35] of Kabir, I have seen it in Kumarji. I have experienced this on two or three occasions. What is this *shūnya*? [*Her eyes close for a moment*] I'm telling you, this is a matter of experience. He was on stage, he began to sing *nirguṇ*, and I had the experience that in these *svaras* I have lost my entire identity. My identity just isn't there. There is only the sound (*svara*), the voice. I have somehow gone, following him, into that aloneness. I have had this experience, and other people have had it too. What is called *shūnya* is a matter of experience. It doesn't happen with other singers, but with Kumar Sahib. I may sing Kumar Sahib's *bhajans*, but what was within Kumar Sahib, that carefreeness, is very difficult to get within myself. . . . He was the emperor of *svaras*. When he was carried away in the *svaras*, in that condition, when he said Kabir's words, he became free of all cares. He became Kabir (Virmani 2004d).

While all music may have the power to take us 'beyond ourselves' in some general sense, there is ample evidence that Kumarji himself, and his close associates, understood *nirguṇ* singing as something particular. This is clear in Kumarji's comments on the wandering Nath who sang '*Suntā hai guru gyānī*'. The next section further explores the quality of voice that expresses what is empty or boundless. As his wife Vasundhara says in that discussion, it is very different from both *saguṇ* and classical.

'*Suntā hai guru gyānī*' is one of the two songs in this collection that I have found most difficult to translate (the other is '*Shūnya gaḍh shahar*'). In both, poet and singer linger in emptiness. In both, the refrain, repeated and explored, is so beautiful and captivating that the listener does not necessarily care if s/he understands all the verses. It is enough to get the mood and the fragments of haunting imagery.

In a conversation once, Kalapini said of this elusive poem, 'In the first line you feel you're touching something, it's nearly in your hand. But it doesn't come to your hand. You always feel that something is there, but when you reach for it, it's not there. There is some mystery, the *guru gyānī* hears it, but we can't.'

At times I have left the translation purposely obscure, letting the images appear unexplained, even unconnected.[36] With music, it becomes connected. The stanzas all illuminate the refrain. In the first three stanzas, there is a movement back and forth between earth and another place. Something subtle happens, then something coalesces on earth (water in one verse, curd in another). In the last three stanzas, one who has seen these distinctions enters into an experience that goes beyond them.

The song gets more and more subtle as it proceeds, more and more empty. The music carries it, the singer's voice silvers it together. His repetition of the refrain, of the words *jhīnī* and *gyānī*, brings us home again and again. The remarkable thinness of the voice at certain points conveys to us the extreme subtlety, the near-insubstantiality, of the image conveyed. *Jhīnī* is sung in this slender way. In the fourth stanza, *bina dhartī ek maṇḍal dīse*—the voice conveys that this almost cannot be said. It is followed by everything dissolving in light.

Yet when everything is gone, something is present. A sound. An instrument. Breath. At the convergence of three streams flies a flag—empty. Nothing on it; it flies.

Gagan meṅ āvāz ho rahī jhīnī jhīnī

A VOICE VIBRATES IN THE SKY, SUBTLE, SUBTLE

In his 1976 interview, Kumarji uses a particular verb for bringing forth the *nirguṇ* voice: *phenknā*—literally, to throw or to hurl. It conveys a more vivid physicality than the English word 'project'; yet 'project' is also apt, for the voice is figured as a kind of projectile. Another meaning of *phenknā* is to shoot or fire—as in shooting an arrow or firing a bullet. The *nirguṇ* voice is thrown, or shot, with great power but, strangely, it does not substantially strike anything. Still, it is effective. This reminds me of verses from a Malwi folk bhajan attributed to Kabir—an *ulatbānsī*, or 'upside-down-language song' that plays with paradoxes and absurdities:

> The hunter picked up his bow and went out. The bow had no string.
> He shot the deer, the deer fell down, but it wasn't hurt.

He brought back the meat of the dead deer
and got a big cheer.

When Kumarji says of the wandering Nath Panthi's singing, 'No one is there,' I imagine that he means not only no listeners but also no singer. When Kabir playfully shows us a deer, shot by a stringless bow, who falls down dead without getting hurt, we are strolling in the vicinity of *shūnya*. 'Throw, but it doesn't hurt.' At least, it doesn't hurt in any conventional sense. Kabir's poetry is full of references to being struck and wounded but differently so, for the 'weapon'—figured as an arrow or other sharp object—is the *shabda*, the word, the guru's voice, the bhajan. This is expressed in '*Lāgī hoy so jāne jo shabad kī*'—a bhajan sung often by Malwa folksingers and rarely by Kumarji:

In the street walks a wounded person
but you can't see the wound with your eyes.
An arrow shot from the bow of wisdom
has lodged in his heart.

A *sākhī* of Kabir conveys this pungently:

Satguru chale shikhār pe, hāth meṇ lāl kabān
murakh murakh bach gaye, koī mārā sant sujān.

The true guru went out hunting,
a red bow in his hand.
Many fools escaped.
Now and then, a true seeker was hit.[37]

In a 2002 conversation, Kumarji's family members spoke with me and Krishna Kant Shukla about the *phenk* of the voice in *nirguṇ* singing.[38]

TAI (VASUNDHARA). First he was attracted to the *nirguṇī svara*. Later he became interested in the literature. . . .

KRISHNA. My understanding is that *nirguṇ svara* means a special way of doing *sā re ga ma* . . .

TAI. Yes, it's about how the *svaras* are thrown. Classical *svaras* are different from *nirguṇ svaras*.

LINDA. Can you say more about it?

TAI. How can I say anything? I can only show you by singing. It has to do with how you project the voice (*uchchāraṇ phenknā*). That is *nirguṇ*. It's not classical. *Saguṇ* is also very different. In *saguṇ*, you know, there's a picture, a person. However you think about God, it appears that way in *saguṇ*. In *nirguṇ* there's no picture, no form. It's without outline, without substance (*nirākār, amurt*). In *nirguṇ svaras*, there's no outline. It's all in the *phenk*. It's all in the way of throwing that *svara*. . . .

LINDA. What kind of practice should be done to achieve that *nirguṇ svara*?

Everyone laughs.

TAI. That is very difficult! It is difficult not only for ordinary people, but for singers like us. . . . I try to experience that *nirguṇ*. I try. I haven't reached the high level that Kumarji reached. That *phenk*. I try.

KALAPINI. So many students of Kumarji have attempted to just sing at least one *svara* in Gandharvaji's style, so that it will be *nirguṇ*. Many people have tried, but it is almost impossible to catch that *svara*. . . . I have just started to sing *nirguṇ bhajans*. I need more time. If Tai is still trying, what can I say? This is a long process. If I sing those words, those *svaras*, with 100 per cent honesty. . . . Imagine the words of '*Nirbhay nirguṇ*'. Do I really experience the meaning of those words? To do 100 per cent justice to the words, we have to keep trying. Not once, not one thousand or two thousand times. We have to keep trying to the end of our lives.

People familiar with Kumarji's singing have often referred to his silences—a unique way of leaving empty space among the syllables and phrases. Vajpeyi illuminates this quality in one of his prose-poems, '*Anupasthitī khiltā hai*', 'Absence blooms':

> Not everything should be filled. Some things should be left empty. Often he stops suddenly, unexpectedly. In the series of notes he leaves an empty space. The space may be empty, but he is present. In empty space, absence blooms (1999: 20).

People sometimes opine that Kumarji's pauses occurred because he had lost the use of one lung and therefore needed to rest and breathe more frequently. Menon denies this:

> Many of his listeners believed that the short, heavily-charged spurts of singing and pause that Kumar favored was the consequence of not having enough breath with which to sing on account of his illness. This was not true. Kumar's breath was sufficient for himself and his musical needs. The seeming pauses in his style of singing was [*sic*] a waiting, in order to make sure that the musical idea he was wishing to convey had duly registered . . . (2001: 79–80).

Kumarji's affinity with *nirguṇ* is naturally traced to his illness—a six-year period of intimacy with death, silence and listening. But a story that long predates the illness gives insight into his discovery of vast space and silence in sound. Sound and silence (like life and death) are not opposites—are not even separate. When Kumarji was still a young teenager, his guru brought him to a legendary elderly woman singer, Anjani Bai Malpekar, and asked her to teach him. She gradually revealed to him secrets of *svara* that he had not glimpsed previously.

Indian musicians speak of *svara* (or *sur*) *sādhanā*—a spiritual practice based on entering the mysterious depths of any given sonic 'location'. If we translate *svara* as a musical tone or note on the scale, we will be technically on the right track, but still far from appreciating its meaning. A 'note' in Indian music is not just a particular spot to be hit accurately, not a line to stick to, but a deep space to which one gains access through an opening of the self. It becomes possible to enter that space after giving up conventional self-consciousness, allowing the voice to merge with something that seems to be already there.[39]

Once I had an experience that helped me appreciate the difference between a note and a *svara*. My friend, classical singer Tara Kini, was giving me some elementary exercises in singing. She turned on the electronic tanpura, gave me a *sā*, and told me to sing it without wavering, not going above or below it. Of course this was beyond my abilities. I tried and failed a number of times. I was tense, trying to hit the note accurately, then trying to hold it in what I pictured mentally as a straight line. One time, unexpectedly, I relaxed and forgot myself. Sound seemed to be coming out of me without my willing it. Surprisingly, it was wide, not narrow. I seemed to be in a space where different threads of sound mingled peacefully and effortlessly to become *sā*. It was startling for me to discover how unlinear a 'note' was.

Anjani Bai Malpekar opened the practice of *svara sādhanā* to the young Kumar Gandharva. Menon reports how Kumarji reminisced, decades later, on his experience with this remarkable woman teacher:

> Anjani Bai had apparently suggested to Kumar to imagine every Swara of the scale as about an inch broad, and if a voice while singing a note would just touch one or the other side of the breadth of this imagined inch, that voice would be considered to sound perfectly *Surela* [in tune]. But if it could be vividly imagined that there was an inch of space between the two edges of the single Swara, it is in this space that the elusive power of the Swara resides. Also, if by sheer persistence a student should find six resting places for his voice within the space of a single note, that singer need never to sing again. It would be the first internal experience of the closest approximation of the Nada Brahman. . . . There is little doubt that in the years following this . . . discovery Kumar persisted in his search for the limitless landscape hidden within a single Swara. And in all probability the humming sound that Krishna Nambiar reports to have heard in the vicinity of Kumar's bed was this soundless inner work which is able to bore a passage through the unfelt inner barriers of a person and reach the very substance of his life (ibid.: 73-5).[40]

Here Menon comes closer to the meaning of those 'spurts and pauses'. One who doesn't know the nature of silence, he quotes Kumarji as saying, can neither speak nor sing. Singing is 'built on the substance of silence . . . at the very centre of every Swara there is hidden a vast . . . silence' (ibid.: 75).

Nirbhay nirguṇ
FEARLESS FORMLESS

Before concluding this introduction, I would like to speak a little of my own experience in listening to Kumar's Kabir. In '*Gurujī ne diyo amar nām*', the speaker celebrates the generosity of one who would give such a precious gift as the 'name', which stands for the word, the sound, the voice, that reveals itself to be a limitless treasure:

Gurujī ne diyo amar nām, guru to sarikhā koī nāhīṅ
Alakh bharyā hai bhandār, kamī jāme hai nāhīṅ

The guru has given me a deathless name.
There is no one like my guruji,
an unseen storehouse, always full,
where there is no lack at all.

In one stanza, the poet is troubled at the thought of giving such a gift to one who doesn't understand its value:

Nām sarikhā jo dān mat dijo ajān ne
Ghughu dekhe tārā [āndhī] jyot, vo kaī jāṇe bhāṇ ne[41]

Don't give a gift like the name
to an ignorant person.
A foolish owl may see starlight
but never know the sun.

I am an unlikely person to write about Kumar Gandharva. I have no expertise in classical Indian music or any music. Even today, it is difficult for me to listen to Kumarji's classical performances since I can't make out *rāga* or *tāla*. From various directions—Kabir, my friends and advisors, the bhajans themselves—I was drawn into this project, wanting to do it, though aware of my limitations. In the process, Kumarji has affected me deeply as he has so many others. I would like to express something of my personal experience by referring to two bhajans that I was able to listen to one day in the Komkali household.

'*Nirbhay nirguṇ*' seems to fly in my consciousness like the banner that appears in its last stanza. When I first heard it on the Triveni recording, its immense energy immediately drew me in, as did that tantalizing juxtaposition in the refrain: fearless formless. 'Boundless' might be a better translation for *nirguṇ* here, but I have used 'formless' with 'fearless' to approximate the sound echo in the original. In this song, *nirguṇ* is wedded to fearlessness. Kumarji sings together with Vasundharaji. Their performance is powerful and inspiring, especially to a fearful person like me. When I first heard the song, I wanted to adopt it, tuck it into my belt, keep it as a mascot.

The Triveni rendition is only four minutes long. In 2002, the Komkali family let me listen to a private concert recording, a much longer exploration of the song. The following year, I asked them to play it again for me. As it began, my body instinctively moved from chair to floor. I closed my eyes. Kumarji's voice intertwined with Vasundharaji's. The song had so much energy, I felt like I was being hit by a high wind. *Nirbhay, nirbhay*! The word 'fearless' is emphasized in many repetitions. There's a mood of exultation, joy and freedom that would be impossible to imagine from just reading the words. The words are about taking a certain yogic posture and doing the practice of reversing the breath, bringing the energy of right and left channels together in the central channel, and attaining an experience of full awakening. It is a common theme in *nirguṇ* poetry. This particular text is a little more technical than most, starting with a statement that the speaker is binding the root lotus in a particular yogic posture. It goes on with stabilizing the mind and uniting the five elements. Reading about it is not necessarily moving.

But the song!

I, and perhaps many others, sometimes harbour a fantasy of spiritual liberation that is devoid of feeling. We have some idea that one would be calm and detached in that *nirguṇ* experience. But in Kumar Gandharva's rendering we discover that *nirguṇ* means *nirbhay*, and *nirbhay* means joyful and free. One is so free that one's joy cannot be contained—it is boundless.

This is also the nature of *nirguṇ*. It is the habit of the mind to be fearful, to cling to its boundaries and definitions. To lose them would be to lose one's identity. Naturally, we're terrified of that. But long before we get to that point, we're scared of losing our jobs, our lovers, our favourite shirts. It is normal to be fearful and clinging. The dissolving of boundaries, however it may happen, is automatically the dissolving of fear. *Nirguṇ* is *nirbhay*. This song arises out of that experience of being formless and fearless. It does not just say I *am* fearless and formless but something more exuberant: I will *sing* the fearless-formless. I will sing a *form* that is fearless-formless. *Nirbhay nirguṇ guṇ re gāūngā, gāūngā, gāūngā*. Three times they repeat the verb: 'I will sing! sing! sing!'

Listening to the song that day, tears came to my eyes. When this happens, a physical change comes over me and I feel blessed. Then, in an act of intuitive kindness and wisdom, Kalapini said, 'There's something else I want you to listen to.' We were not in those lovely spaces of the house where Kumarji's presence is palpable—the drawing room with his tanpuras in glass-doored cabinets; the room where he slept and practised music, with a small shrine holding his smiling picture; the front veranda with the wide swing where he loved to sit, looking out on the garden—but in the office, a small, efficient space featuring the computer and speakers with which Bhuvan works with old recordings, preserving and restoring them.

Kalapini started the piece she wanted me to hear, then went out and left me alone. It was a version of '*Sakhiyā vā ghar sab se nyārā*'—again a private recording, not the one that is available in the market. This purely *nirguṇ* song, which proceeds by an accumulation of negations, is very different from '*Nirbhay nirguṇ*'. It is sung in utter simplicity and calm.

I had just worked on the translation. The verbal structure is very common in *nirguṇ* poetry: There's no day or night, no sun or moon, inside or outside, good or bad, etc., *there*, in that place which is *nyārā*. Here is a description of what happened to me as I listened that day, written down a few days later, in the present tense:

> His voice is so plain and simple—hard to believe it is coming from an artist of infinite skill. He sings very slowly and deliberately with lots

> of space in the sound. I feel this voice, so quiet and calm, is coming inside my body and stirring me irresistibly. It stirs inside me, and a hard crust that is like a body within my body begins to come apart. It just comes apart and dissolves. What is underneath it is so pure and shining and open, it can receive that beautiful sound with no resistance. What was closed is open. The sound moves freely in my body, the beautiful body that shines forth when the crust dissolves. I can't believe that this gift is being given to me. When it's over I can't talk. They ask me to come to lunch, but when I put my hand on the food, I can't eat. I go into the other room and cry till it seems to be enough. I'm full of gratitude and amazement. It seems to me that for the first time I understand what they mean here when they say 'the guru's grace'. This gift comes into you and changes you. It is completely unexpected.

Milo nirguṇ se
MEET WITH NIRGUN

Jab maiṅ thā tab hari nahīṅ, ab hari hai maiṅ nāhīṅ
prem galī ati sānkarī, yāme do samāye nāhīṅ

When I was here, God was gone.
Now God is here, I'm gone.
The lane of love is very narrow.
Two can't go in.

This is Kabir's *sākhī*. Sometimes his imagery runs toward love, though *nirguṇ* love would have to be a strange thing. People writing and talking about Kumarji often say that listening to him produced one of the great experiences of their lives; it took them beyond themselves.

The phrase *milo nirguṇ se* comes with Kabir's signature in a folk version of *'Ham pardesī panchhī bābā'*. It is a contradiction: you can't meet with *nirguṇ*. Yet the poet-singer gives this assignment, leaving us to make of it what we will.

Kabir hovers at the juncture of two / one, yes / no, form / emptiness, not taking sides.

Hāṅ kahūṅ to hai nahīṅ, nā kahā nahīṅ jāī
Hāṅ aur nā ke bīch meṅ, morā satguru rahā samāī

If I say yes, it isn't so,
and I can't say no.
Between yes and no a space,
my true guru's place.[42]

The deathless, the *amar nām*, exists exactly amidst *nashvartā*, the perishable, where time runs, nothing stays the same, where *shūnya* is in the pauses and the old *bandish* is born now.

We may notice *shūnya* in the pauses. Later, we understand that *shūnya* is also in the *svaras*.

Taking off from the *sākhī* about the narrow lane of love, Ashok Vajpeyi imagines a meeting between K and K:

The lane was narrow and two couldn't pass at once.
But there were two in that lane,
one from centuries back and one from today.
(The lane of love is outside of time.)
From one came words, from the other voice,[43]
there near Shiva's shrine.
When the weaver came with his one-stringed instrument
it was difficult even for him to know
who was who.
For a moment in that lane they appear separate.
Then they merge
like this:
the shadow of one
and the shadow of the other
cannot stay apart.

(1999: 24)

Notes

1 I have heard a Malwi folk version of the well-known Kabir song '*Yā ghaṭ bhītar*' sung by P. S. Tipanya, and a classical version in a variant form ('*Is ghaṭ antar*') composed and sung by Shubha Mudgal. A version of the text appears in the collection at the end of Hazariprasad Dvivedi's famous book, *Kabīr* (1961). Gulammohammed Sheikh's series of paintings *Kahat Kabir* includes one that he called *Yā ghaṭ bheetar*. Though Kumarji did not sing this song, the theme of finding the whole universe and the key to truth in the body, figured as a clay pot (*ghaṭ*), is omnipresent in Kabir and other *nirguṇ* poetry. For example, in this volume, see '*Guruji maiṅ to ek niranjan dhyāūṅ jī*' (I meditate only on the one; p. 110), *and* '*Kāchī chhe kāyā thārī*' (Your body is an unbaked clay pot, p. 114).

2 Two species of Indian cuckoo famed for their beautiful singing, often appearing in poetry to symbolize enchanting music and deep devotion.

3 *Rasiktā* is difficult to translate. *Ras* is the juice or essence of deep aesthetic emotion. A *rasik* is one who is capable of experiencing *ras*. *Rasiktā* is the noun: the quality of one who is able to experience profound artistic feeling.

4 There is a famous temple to Goddess Chamunda on a hilltop in Dewas. The Kumar Gandharva house is on *Mātājī kā rāstā* (Mother's Road), which goes up that hill. (E. M. Forster's memoir of time spent in Dewas is named *The Hill of Devi* [1953].)

5 The full moon, *purnima* in the month of Ashadh (mid-June to mid-July), according to the Hindu calendar, is traditionally celebrated as Guru Purnima by Hindus. Also known as Vyas Purnima, the day is celebrated in remembrance and veneration to Ved Vyas—the *adi* (original) guru who, according to tradition, classified the Vedas, wrote the 18 Puranas and the Mahabharata. On this day, all gurus are meant to be paid tribute by their disciples/devotees.

6 *Bandish*: musical composition, often to a text.

7 The Malwi folk version by P. S. Tipanya has *sīnchanahārā*, 'one who waters'. Shubha Mudgal's version has *sirjanahārā*, 'the creator'.

8 See NOTE 1.

9 Both of these passages are from Kabir bhajans I have learned from folksinger P. S. Tipanya: the first quotation is from '*Rām rame soī gyānī*' [One who revels in Ram is the true wise one], the second from '*Begam kī gam kar le re hansā*' [Nowhere, go there, oh swan]. Tipanya sings another bhajan that simultaneously captures the wondrous beauty and the poignant transiency of the body:

> Come to the guru's country, let me show you the city of love.
> Like the young buds of the *kachinar* tree, a craftsman has made this wondrous body . . .
> The golden moth flies away at the moment of death . . .
> Don't be proud of your body, it's a bag of skin, full of flaws . . .
> Bhavaninath says, through these songs my body was transformed.
> Come to the guru's country, let me show you the city of love.

10 For discussions of the knotty problems of Kabir's textual traditions, see Vaudeville (1993), Hess (1987), Callewaert et al. (2000) and Dharwadker (2003). I am working on a new study of Kabir oral traditions and their relation to written / recorded traditions. For collections of Kabir's poetry in English translation, see Vaudeville (1993), Dharwadker (2003) and Hess (2002).

11 Sunil Mukhi, an admirer of Kumar Gandharva, has created a website on Kumarji at theory.tifr.res.in/~mukhi/Music/gandharva.html.

12 On the gharana tradition and Kumarji's relation to it, see Ashok Vajpeyi's 'Passing Away' in this volume.

13 See theory.tifr.res.in/~mukhi/Music/gandharva.html

14 This section heading, like most of the others, is based on a phrase from a Kabir bhajan. 'Words without edges' here represents *anahad bāṇī* in the song '*Avadhūtā kudrat kī gat nyārī*'. *Anahad* means, literally, 'without boundary'; *bāṇī* means 'word'. Kabir-*bāṇī* is a general term for the utterances of Kabir, the body of his compositions. Most listeners would also associate *bāṇī* with *shabda* (word) and *nād* (sound)—the mysterious auditory experience of ultimate reality, evoked in the term *anahad nād*, unstruck sound.

15 This entire bhajan can be heard online at www.musicindia

online.com. Type in Kumar Gandharva as a search term and select '*Udai* [sic] *hans akela*' under the heading 'Devotional'.

16 In his landmark 1942 book *Kabīr*, Hindi literary scholar Hazariprasad Dvivedi suggests that the weavers of Varanasi, like other artisan communities, might have converted as a group to Islam around the fourteenth century, and that Kabir's family was likely to have been affiliated before and perhaps after conversion with the householder branch of the Nath Panth, a sect that followed yogic traditions, popular and influential during this period in the region.

17 Hindus normally cremate the dead, but religious renunciants and persons regarded as holy are often buried. The pit was to be a burial place.

18 This story was told to me by Krishna Kant Shukla in 2002.

19 Kumarji's disciple Madhup Mudgal gives a moving account of this moment in a film interview which appears in Shabnam Virmani's documentary *Koi Sunta Hai / Someone is Listening: Journeys with Kumar and Kabir* (2008ii).

20 Here is Vajpeyi's vivid description of the setting, atmosphere, and tone of this long conversation:

> Even if it hadn't been a rainy day, Kumar Gandharva's Dewas home, Bhanukul, where this conversation took place, would have had that sort of pale, soft darkness combined with pale, soft brightness. And there would have been that sense of affectionate peacefulness that we associate with Kumar Gandharva's music. His house, surrounded on all sides with greenery, had none of that kind of showy wealth which makes the eyes feel uneasy. Nor did it have the atmosphere of a mansion that belongs to a musical lineage, or the sort of glittering grandness one often finds among Indian musicians who have attained international fame. There were tanpuras and tablas put away with great care—including those left-hand drums on which Kumarji used to prop his elbow—and everything announced an ordinary life in a house that had such a sense of gentleness and intimacy that one immediately had a desire to stay there. Even when someone was joining the conversation for the first time, the house felt very familiar, as if one had been there often.

Kumar Gandharva was waiting for his interviewers in this prearranged session. Most of the questions had been prepared in advance, but in the course of five hours some new ones arose, and at certain points the conversation began to turn into a debate. Out of concern about excessive length, and to retain the form of the conversation, these parts have been removed. Perhaps because his first language is Kannada, Kumar Gandharva speaks Hindi very fast; and because his second language is Marathi, he uses many Marathi words. His Hindi is interesting to listen to. It comes out in bits of sentences, and often, after speaking a half sentence, he will finish it by curving his body in a certain way, or with a silence. This manner of speaking naturally can't come across in a printed piece, and a number of important points have therefore had to be cut. But while editing, we have done our best to insure that Kumar Gandharva's way of conversing, even if dimmed, does not disappear entirely (1999: 83–4).

21 Gorakhnath is revered as the founder of the Nath Panth. Machhinder, a dialectal form of Matsyendra, is believed to have been Gorakhnath's guru. Guesses about their dates range from the eighth to the twelfth centuries.

22 I am very grateful to my friend Krishna Kant Shukla who let me borrow his precious copy of the book and get it photocopied in 2002. In 2006, I heard that the Shilnāth Dhūnī Sansthān had produced a new edition.

23 Shilnath reference numbers are given in notes to the translations.

24 Kumarji also composed and sang '*Ramaiyyā kī dulhin lūṭā bāzār*', but it did not make as great an impact as '*Māyā mahāthaganī*'.

25 Part of this passage appears in Virmani (2008ii).

26 *Sākhī* 120 (Singh 1972: 158).

27 A synonym for *sen* is *sanket*, the word Krishna Nath reports Kumarji to have used in talking about the source of music.

28 On what would have been Kumar Gandharva's 83rd birthday in April 2006, Gautam Chatterjee wrote a reminiscence of attending a performance in April 1991, Kumarji's last visit to Varanasi. On that occasion, Chatterjee says, he sang '*Shūnya gaḍh shahar*' for the first time and discussed it in an interview:

We were all celebrating his 68th birthday on April 8, 1991, in Varanasi at the Krishnamurthy Foundation. He had come here to express his feelings musically at the Sankat Mochan Sangeet Samaroh. It turned out to be his last performance [in that city], for he passed away on January 12, 1992. Even as admirers of Pandit Kumar Gandharva listened to him for the last time, the musical genius was presenting them something new: his own creation, raga Malawati, with a bhajan of Gorakhanath '*Shunya garh shahar, shahar ghar basti*' . . .

One could see that in spite of his breaking breaths, the familiar magic of his voice over all three octaves, was as harmonious as he was known for. He was with his young daughter Kalapini. After explaining a folktale about birthday celebrations in Marathi to my friend Kalyani Khairnar, who was translating part of the interview, Kumarji unpredictably started a discussion on the two key words 'Avadhuta' and 'Shunya'. His eyes rested on the cover of J. Krishnamurthy's famous book *Freedom from the Known* and elaborated on why he always chose the verses of Kabir more than those of Surdas and Meerabai, and why he was going to sing the words of Gorakh in the place of Kabir. . . .

He said, 'Saint Kabir derived the mystic language, which is popularly known as upside-down language or Sandhya Bhasha, from the language of Nathpanthis like Matsyendra Nath and Gorakh Nath. I have already sung a pada of Gorakh, "*Bhola Mana Jane Ye Amara Meri Kaya*" [The childish mind is sure: my body is immortal] where I found the immense capacity of Shunya and the capability to make the space of Shunya in singing. Almost all the Nirgunapanthis create a Shunya when they sing a bhajan. What is this, I have been thinking about this abstract singing from my adolescent days. . . .

'And finally I found,' his eyes sparkled and he put aside the book, 'it is where I am. Actually the Nirgunapanthis throw this Shunya or throw this word in an upside-down manner to create the Shunya.

'I cannot be as expert as they are but at this time, only this interests me, attracts me. So to create a feeling of Shunya without words within me, I usually sing these padas of Kabir and here, I decided on Gorakh to move a step . . . towards the root, towards the previous time of Kabir.

'This pada "*Shunya Garha Shahar* . . ." is addressed to Shunya itself. That is the only beauty of this pada and the destiny where I am to move finally.'

29 Discussing this bhajan with me, Vasundhara and Bhuvan Komkali said that it has an unusual potency; they used the words *bhārī* (heavy, intense) and *nashā* (intoxication) and their gestures indicated a movement of energy rising to the head—*Māthā garam hotā hai*, they said, 'the head gets hot.'

30 P. S. Tipanya sings this song with Kabir's signature line.

31 When I asked Tara Kini whether I was right to say he goes into a minor key, she explained in Indian musical terms, 'Yes, he suddenly goes into *komal svaras*' on this syllable.

32 The verb for singing here is *sunānā*, literally, 'to cause to hear'. This is the causative form of *sunnā*, to hear.

33 For example, the famous thirteenth-century Sanskrit treatise on music, *Sangītaratnākara*, theorizes the production of audible sound from the primordial *nāda*, with detailed reference to the body and to the categories of yogic practice:

> We worship nada-brahman, that incomparable bliss which is immanent in all the creatures as intelligence and is manifest in the phenomenon of this universe. Indeed, through the worship of nada are worshipped gods (like) Brahma, Visnu and Siva, since essentially they are one with it. . . . The vital force stationed around the root of the navel, rising upwards gradually manifests nada in the navel, the heart, the throat, the cerebrum, and the cavity of the mouth as it passes through them. . . . Stationed in these five places, nada takes on five different names as associated with them respectively, viz., extremely subtle, subtle, loud, not-so-loud and artificial. . . . It is understood that the syllable na . . . represents the vital force and da represents fire . . . Nada is differentiated into twenty-two grades which, because of their audibility, are known as sruti-s. [The sruti-s are associated with nadi-s or subtle energy channels in the body.] . . . From out of the sruti-s arise the svara-s; these are seven, viz., sadja, rsabha, gandhara, madhyam, pancama, dhaivata and nisada. . . . another accepted nomenclature is 'sa-ri-ga-ma-pa-dha-ni' . . . Immediately consequent upon sruti, creamy and resonating, the

sound that delights the listeners' minds by itself is called svara (Sringy and Sharma 1999: 108–35).

34 It would be more accurate to refer to Nath Panthis, as Kabir Panthis are generally settled householders, not homeless wanderers.

35 She uses the term *phakkarpan*, which was also used by Kumarji in the passage just quoted. Perhaps she had seen his interview. She speaks of *ekānt*, 'aloneness', as he does, but uses the term Kabir Panthis where Kumarji speaks of Nath Panthis.

36 See notes to the translation for explanation of some of the yogic meanings.

37 *Sākhī* learned orally from P. S. Tipanya. A folk bhajan that beautifully shows the double meaning of being shot by the arrow of the guru's word is Tipanya's '*Mhārā satgurū baniyā bhediyā*'—my true guru became my *bhediyā*. *Bhediyā* means 'one who reveals the mystery', *bhed*, but the verb *bhednā* also means 'to penetrate' or 'pierce'. One stanza says of the guru:

He aimed his spear
and it struck my heart.
He wounded me!
He gave me vision
in the middle
of my body.
Syllables burst
into light.

38 The conversation, on 13 March 2002, took place in Kumar Gandharva–Komkali home in Dewas. Participants were Vasundhara Komkali (called Tai), Kalapini Komkali, Bhuvanesh Komkali, my friend (also a singer and devotee of Kumar Gandharva) Krishna Kant Shukla of Varanasi and myself.

39 'The basic unit of the Indian scale is the Swara and not the Western note which is based on the frequencies of a tuning fork. The Swara on the other hand is a personal utterance. . . . Broken down to its Sanskrit roots, the root Swa refers to the inner self of the student, and the root Ra which refers to the shining out of this inner self. In combination the word Swara would mean the radiance of the inner

self and this is the essence of the Swara . . .' (Menon 2001: 36–8).

40 One more memorable image of the *svara* that Menon passes on: 'Kumar once said . . . for students of music in Delhi a few years before his passing: . . . "You must think of a Swara as though it were a fish. It can go straight ahead along the scale, or swim in the same place at various depths. If you do not go ahead there [are] . . . plenty of places where you are on the same note at different levels" ' (2001.: 97).

41 See notes in song translations.

42 *Sākhī* learned orally from P. S. Tipanya.

43 The poem says: from one came *shabda*, from the other *svara*. The reader will now appreciate the depth of these terms, impossible to transport adequately into an English translation.

ABOUT THE TEXTS AND TRANSLATIONS

There is no such thing as a perfect oral text. The bhajans sung by Kumar Gandharva appear with slight variations in different sources, which include the programmes he distributed at concerts, the *Shīlnāth Śhabdāmṛit*, the family's records of his texts and different performances by him. Publishing this book will create a kind of canonical version of Kumar Gandharva's *nirguṇ* bhajans, but canons are made to be challenged and interested readers will find discrepancies.

My procedure has been to seek out any existing written versions of the text, then to listen to sung versions and correct any obvious inconsistencies, often consulting with other listeners. The main, publicly available, written texts are those that Kumar Gandharva provided in printed programmes for his audiences, and those that are in the Shilnath book. Friends who are familiar with the bhajans have checked the texts and made suggestions. In the last stages of preparing this book, I was able to sit with Bhuvan Komkali, Kumar Gandharva's grandson, who compared the texts I had with Kumarji's notebooks and made corrections. Notes to each bhajan indicate sources of the text as well as references to folk versions that I am familiar with.

Any published version of a text tends to get privileged and fixed. The printed programmes that Kumarji prepared for many of his concerts are precious resources for us now. But they are not totally reliable. For example, in the programme of *Saguṇ Nirguṇ Bāṇī*, the song '*Gurā to jī ne gyān kī jaḍiyā daī*' (The guru has given a root of wisdom) has a refrain and three stanzas. But in Kumarji's recorded versions, there is another stanza which comes as the second of four (*pāncho nāg pachchīso nāganī* . . .). This bhajan is often sung by Malwi folk singers, and the 'missing stanza' is always in their versions. So we should have it here.

There are canonical performances as well as texts. Kumarji will have sung a particular bhajan many times, but the performance or studio recording that gets into a published album becomes canonized. Whatever little things he did with his voice on that occasion, his pauses, repetitions, ornamentations, rises and falls, will become the text that we, poor intellectuals, pore over and analyse.

If questions arise even about the basic Hindi text, what of translation? From morning to afternoon, I change my mind about what would be the best word, syntax, or line-break in the English version. Though I must take responsibility for the choices that get frozen in this book, it is still a good idea for all of us—readers, singers, listeners, translators—to imagine this as a fluid process. If the oral tradition teaches us anything, it is that each encounter is new and personal. As Kumar Gandharva, in his 50s, said before singing a composition: 'I learned this when I was eight. But it will be born now.' Folksingers change the words of a bhajan as it moves from one person, place or performance to another. You too can change the words of my translations.

Another point worth mentioning is that a text on a page will often seem pale and disappointing to someone who knows that text as part of a glorious musical performance. A translation is likely to fare even worse. One or two evocative lines can make a song unforgettable: the melody, expression and keywords are so powerful that the listener can gloss over obscure and difficult lines, carried away by music and mood. The translator cannot.

People who know both Hindi and English, lovers of Kumar Gandharva who are familiar with these songs, are likely to disagree with many points in the translation. But to encounter the written Hindi texts with the English versions and notes, and to reflect on why they disagree and what might be a better rendition, may stimulate new consciousnesses and connections. I have met many people who know and love Kumarji's *nirguṇ* bhajans. Most have said the words are not 100 per cent clear to them. Either his Marathi / Kannada-tinged pronunciation or just the difficulty of the texts themselves may stand in the way of full understanding. So I hope that even dissatisfaction with my translations will (like the irritant in an oyster that produces a pearl) give rise to more beautiful and intimate relationships with the songs.

A SPECIAL RECORDING

The first edition of *Singing Emptiness*, published in 2009, included a very special CD that had been created for the book. As we prepare the new edition, in 2021, the technology of physical CDs has become a thing of the past. Yet the CD that accompanied *Singing Emptiness* has been widely appreciated and shared. Given the likelihood that its contents will continue to be shared among individuals and through media, we include the description and acknowledgements originally published in the book.

Some of the *nirguṇ* bhajans that Kumarji sang have never become available to the public. Others, while once in the market, are now difficult to find. Inspired by U. R. Ananthamurthy, I dreamed that a set of new recordings might be issued with this book. That dream came true, thanks to the generosity and efforts of the Komkali family and others. Vasundhara Komkali gave her blessings, Kalapini worked out the details with me over a number of meetings, and Bhuvanesh's expertise produced high-quality versions of recordings originally made in live performances where equipment and conditions were less than perfect. The encouragement and support of Ashok Vajpeyi and O.P. Jain were indispensable in making the CD come forth.

The five bhajans on the original CD provided, for the first time, a publicly available version of the magnificent and profound *Shūnya gaḍh shahar* (discussed in the introduction, part 4). Also available for the first time was *Maiṅ jāgūṅ mhārā satguru jāge*, which Kumarji evoked in his long interview as embodying the unique world of the wandering yogi, the world and the mind from which the nirguṇ voice could be 'thrown' (introduction, part 5). The other three bhajans had been in the market previously, but in shorter studio-recorded versions, some of which remain hard to find.

For the first time, this CD presented a set of *nirguṇ* bhajans from live performances. Sometimes we can hear responses from the audience, and always we are aware that Kumarji was exploring the music with the kind of immediacy and openness that are more likely to happen in a performance than in a studio. *Naiyā morī*, though at one time available as a bhajan on a cassette devoted mainly to classical compositions, is difficult to find. And when one does encounter it on the internet, the quality cannot compare to the version on our CD. *Māyā mahāṭhaganī*, well known in a shorter version, is here explored at length (see introduction, part 4). *Sakhiyā vā ghar*, in this amazing nineteen-minute version, became especially meaningful to me in the preparation of the book (introduction, part 7).

These bhajans are all drawn from a concert on 12 January 1980, at the home of Shrimati Rajani and Shri Shirish Patel in Mumbai. Accompanying Kumarji are Vasundhara Komkali, vocal; Vasant Achrekar, tabla; and Govind Patwardhan, harmonium.

THE SONGS

This collection of 30 *nirguṇ* song texts is divided into two parts: those with Kabir's signature line (1–21), and those with signatures of others, or with none (22–30). Each section is alphabetical by first line. The *ṭek*, or refrain, is italicized.

SONGS WITH KABIR'S SIGNATURE LINE

1. *Avadhūtā gagan ghaṭa gaharānī*[1]

Oh solitary wanderer, dense stormclouds
gather in the sky.

From the west comes a cloud
upside-down. *Rhum-jhum*
goes the rain. Wake up,
wise one, take care of your field!
The water will flow away!
With absorption and awareness as your bullocks,[2]
sow the seed, your own grain.
Choked by the grass of doubt,[3]
it won't take root.
Sow the grain of the name.
At the four corners, four guards watch
so the deer won't eat the grain.
Harvest the crop, crush it, bring it home—
your farming is complete.
Five women meet and cook
the meal. Sages and wise ones eat.
Kabir says, listen
friend, sow the grain
of the name.[4]

1. *Avadhūtā gagan ghaṭa gaharānī*

अवधूता गगन घटा गहरानी (टेक)
पछ्म दिसा से उलटी बादल, रुम झुम बरसे मेहा
उठो ग्यानी खेत संभारो, बह निसरेगा पानी (१)
निरत सुरत के बेल बनावो, बीज बोवो निज धानी
दुबध्या दूब जमन नहिं पावे, बोवो नाम की धानी (२)
चारो कोने चार रखवाले चुग ना जावे मृग धानी
काट्या खेत मींडा घर लावे, जाकी पूरण किसानी (३)
पांच सखी मिल करे रसोई, जीमे मुनि और ग्यानी
कहे कबीर सुनो भाई साधो, बोवो नाम की धानी (४)

2. Avadhūtā kudrat kī gat nyārī[5]

Oh solitary wanderer, nature's ways are strange.[6]
She turns a beggar to a king,
a king to a beggar.

Cloves grow without fruit,
sandalwood blooms without blooming.
A fish goes hunting in the jungle,
a lion slithers through the ocean,
castor-oil plants turn to fragrant forests,
the scent bursts out in all directions.
The cosmos is carved
into three worlds,
a blind man watches the show.
A lame man leaps
over Mount Sumeru,
swings free
through the three worlds.
A mute illumines
wisdom and knowledge,
speaking an endless word.
The sky is tied and hurled
to the underworld.
A serpent rules heaven.
Kabir says, Ram is king.
Whatever he does
makes sense.[7]

2. *Avadhūtā kudrat kī gat nyārī*

अवधूता कुदरत की गत न्यारी न्यारी
रंक नवाज करे वो राजा, भूपति करे भिकारी (टेक)
येते लवंगहि फल नहीं लागे, चन्दन फूले न फूले
मच्छ शिकारी रमे जंगल में, सिंघ समुद्रहि झूले (१)
रेडा रूख भया मलयागर, चहू दिशी फूटी बसा
तीन लोक ब्रह्मान्ड खंड में, देखे अंध तमाशा (२)
पंगुल मेरू सुमेरू उलंघे, त्रिभुवन मुक्ता डोले
गूंगा ज्ञान विज्ञान प्रकाशे, अनहद बाणी बोले (३)
बांधी आकाश पताल पठावै, शेष स्वर्ग पर राजै
कहे कबीर राम है राजा, जो कछु करे सो छाजै (४)

3. *Avadhūtā yugan yugan ham yogī*[8]

Oh solitary wanderer, for ages and ages
I've been a yogi.

I don't come or go,
never disappear,
enjoying the endless sound.[9]
Everywhere I see my people,
every place a gathering.
I'm in all,
all are in me,
with many, I'm alone.
I'm yogic power,
deep meditation.
I'm silent,
I speak.
Showing outer form,
inner form,
no form,
I play
within myself.
Kabir says, listen friend,
seeker, I have no desire.
In my hut, I sway
in the self. I play
simply to please[10]
myself.

3. *Avadhūtā yugan yugan ham yogī*

अवधूता युगन युगन हम योगी
आवै न जाय मिटै ना कबहुं, सबद अनाहत भोगी (टेक)
सभी ठौर जमात हमारी, सब ही ठौर पर मेला
हम सब माय, सब है हम माय, हम है बहुरी अकेला (१)
हम ही सिद्ध, समाधि हम ही, हम मौनी हम बोले
रूप सरूप अरूप दिखा के, हम ही में हम तो खेले (३)
कहे कबीरा जो सुनो भाई साधो, नाहीं न कोई इच्छा
अपनी मढ़ी में आप में डोलूं, खेलूं सहज स्वइच्छा (४)

4. *Bin satguru nar rahat bhulānā*[11]

Without the true guru, humans are lost.
They search and wander but can't find the way.

A shepherd raised a lion cub,
he cared for him so cleverly.
That cub gambolled with the goats,
not knowing his own nature.
One day a lion came from the jungle,
saw this and lost his temper.
He plucked out the cub and suddenly
showed him the truth. The young lion
smiled.[12] So this is my true state!
Like the musk deer who holds
in his centre
enchanting aroma
but wanders all over
searching like a fool,
he sees his own mind
and comes to rest.[13]
Where does the beautiful fragrance reside?
Between upbreath and downbreath,
concentration, rapturous form,
no description.
Kabir says, listen seeker, friend,
self turns, merges
with self.[14]

4. *Bin satguru nar rahat bhulānā*

बिन सतगुरु नर रहत भुलाना
खोजत फिरत राह नहीं जाना (टेक)
केहर सुत ले आयो गडरिया, पाल पोस उन कीन्ह सयाना
करत कलोल रहत अजयन संग, आपन मर्म उनहुं नहीं जाना (१)
केहर इक जंगल से आयो, ताहि देखि बहुतै रिसियाना
पकड़ि के भेद तुरत समझाया, आपन दशा देखि मुसक्याना (२)
जस कुरंग बिच वसत बासना, खोजत मूढ़ फिरत चौगाना
कर उसवास मनै में देखे, यह सुगंधि धौं कहां बसाना (३)
अर्ध उर्ध बिच लगन लगी है, छक्यो रूप नहीं जात बखाना
कहत कबीर सुनो भाई साधो, उलटि आप में आप समाना (४)

5. *Dhun sun ke manavā magan huā jī*[15]

My mind disappeared
into that melody.

Awareness absorbed
in the guru's feet,
at last, friend, all sorrow
is gone.
From the essence-word, a cord—[16]
the swan rises, crosses
free. On the peak
of emptiness
shimmer of cymbals
rain of nectar
drops of love.
Kabir says, listen friend, seeker,
each taste
gives bliss.[17]

5. *Dhun sun ke manavā magan huā jī*

धुन सुन के मनवा मगन हुआ जी (टेक)
लागी समाधी गुरू चरणा जी अंत सखा दुख दूर हुवा जी
सार शब्द एक डोरी लागी ते चढ़ हंसा पार हुवा जी (१)
शून्य शिखर पर झालर झलके बरसत अमरित प्रेम चुवा जी
कहे कबीरा सुनो भाई साधो चाख चाख अलमस्त हुवा जी (२)

6. *Gurujī ne diyo amar nām*[18]

Guruji has given me a deathless name.
There's no one like my guruji,
an unseen storehouse, always full,
where there is no lack at all.

Don't give a gift like the name
to an ignorant person.
A foolish owl may see starlight[19]
but never know the sun.

Cut it, but it won't be cut.
Burn it, but it won't burn.
Read all the sacred books
but without the guru
you can't get the name.

When the sun rises over earth and water,
the moon and stars disappear.
So yoga and chanting, all your ascetic efforts,
sink before the name.

All thoughts in the mind disappear
as you speak your own name.
Kabir says, the lord is in this body!
Let's go home.

6. *Gurujī ne diyo amar nām*

गुरूजी ने दियो अमर नाम
गुरू तो सरिखा कोई नाहीं
अलख भर्या है भंडार कमी जामे है नहीं (टेक)
नाम सरीखा यो नाम मति दो अजाण ने
घुघु देखे तारा आंधी जोत, वो कंई जाणे भाण ने (१)
खर्चे से ना खुटिया, जलाया से ना जले
बांची वेद पुराण नामे गरु बिना ना मिले (२)
उग्या जल थल भाण चंदा तारा छिप गया
जप तप जोग अनेक नाम तले दबी गया (३)
चित मन चिंता मिट्यो रटो निज नाम ने
घट भीतर साहेब कबीर चलो निज धाम (४)

7. *Ham pardesī panchhī bābā* [20]

I'm a bird from another country, baba,
I don't belong to this country.
The people in this country are unconscious,
every moment sunk in regret,
brothers, seekers, I don't belong
to this country.

I sing without a mouth
walk without feet
fly without wings.
Awareness free
of illusion, I play
in the limitless.

Sitting in shadow, I'm on fire.
In sunlight, I'm cool.
My true guru is beyond
sun and shade.
I dwell in the guru.

Stick to your posture
day and night[21]
but the lord won't come down.
Wise ones and meditators
have worked themselves to death
in that country.

The great giver whose form
is formless
takes on the form
of a name.
Mind and breath
can never reach
that country.

Head, toes, eyes
this body
the true teacher has transformed
beyond death.
Kabir says, listen seekers,
the lord is inside
the body.

7. *Ham pardesī panchhī bābā*

हम परदेसी पंछी बाबा, अणी देसरा नाहीं हो
अणी देस रा लोग अचेता, पल पल पर पछताई भाई संतो
अणी देस रा नाहीं हो (टेक)
मुख बिन गाना पग बिन चलना, बिन पंख उड़ जाई हो
बिना मोह की सुरत हमारी, अनहद में रम जाई (१)
छाया बैठूं अगनी व्यापे, धूप अधिक सितलाई हो
छाया धूप से सतगुरू न्यारा, मैं सतगुरू के माई (२)
आठों पेहेर अड़क रहे आसन, कदे न उतरे शाही
मन पवन दोनों नहीं पहुंचे, उनी देस के माही (३)
निरगुण रूप है मेरे दाता, सरगुण नाम धराई
कहे कबीर सुनो भाई साधो, साहब है घट माही (४)

8. *Hiranā samajh būjh ban charanā*[22]

Deer, be aware,
be wise
when you graze
in the forest.

Graze in the first forest,
graze in the second forest.
don't set foot
in the third forest.

Five hunters live
in the third forest.
Don't let their gaze
fall on you!

Five male deer,
twenty-five female deer,
not one of them
is wise.[23]

They'll kill you and sell your meat,
they'll flay you and use your skin
for a mat.

Kabir says, listen seekers,
Keep your mind
in the guru's feet.

8. *Hiranā samajh būjh ban charanā*

हिरना समझ बूझ बन चरना (टेक)
एक बन चरना, दूजे बन चरना, तीजे बन पग नहीं धरना (१)
तीजे बन में पांच पारधी, उनके नजर नहीं पड़ना (२)
पांच हिरना, पचीस हिरनी, उन में एक चतुर ना (३)
तोय मार तेरी मास बिकावे, तेरे खाल का करेंगे बिछोना (४)
कहे कबीराजी सुनो भाई साधो, गुरु के चरण चित धरना (५)

9. *Jhīnī jhīnī bīnī chadariyā*[24]

Subtle, subtle, subtle
is the weave
of that cloth.

What is the warp
what is the weft
with what thread
did he weave
that cloth?

Right and left
are warp and weft
with the thread at the centre
he wove
that cloth[25]

The spinning wheel whirled
eight lotuses, five elements,
three qualities, he wove
that cloth

It took ten months
to finish the stitching
thok! *thok*! he wove
that cloth

Gods, sages, humans wrapped
the cloth around them
they wrapped it
and got it dirty
that cloth

Kabir wrapped it with such care
that it stayed just as it was

at the start
that cloth.

Subtle, subtle, subtle
is the weave
of that cloth.

9. *Jhīnī jhīnī bīnī chadariyā*

झीनी झीनी झीनी बीनी चदरिया
काहे कै ताना काहे कै भरनी, कौन तार से बीनी चदरिया (टेक)
इंगला पिंगला ताना भरनी, सुखमन तार से बीनी चदरिया (१)
आठ कंवल दल चरखा डोले, पांच तत्त गुन तीनी चदरिया (२)
साई को सियत मास दस लागे, ठोक ठोक कै बीनी चदरिया (३)
सो चादर सुर नर मुनि ओढ़े, ओढ़ के मैली कीनी चदरिया (४)
दास कबीरा जतन से ओढ़े, ज्यों की त्यों धर दीनी चदरिया (५)

10. *Kaun ṭhagavā nagariyā lūṭal ho*[26]

What thief has looted the town?

On a cot made of sandalwood, the bride lay.
Get up, dear friend, adorn the parting
of my hair! The bridegroom is upset with me.
Along came King Death, climbed up on the bed.
Tears broke from eyes.
Four people got together, lifted the cot—
smoke, smoke in all directions.
Kabir says, listen seekers, friends,
all ties to the world
have dropped away.

10. *Kaun ṭhagavā nagariyā lūṭal ho*

कौन ठगवा नगरिया लूटल हो (टेक)
चंदन काठ के बनल खटोला, ता पर दुलहिन सूतल हो (१)
उठो सखी री मांग सवारौ, दुलहा मोसे रूठल हो (२)
आये जमराजा पलंग चढ़ि बैठा, नैनन अंसुवा टूटल हो (३)
चार जने मिल खाट उठाइन, चहुं दिसि घौं घौं उठल हो (४)
कहत कबीरा सुनो भाई साधो, जगसे नाता छूटल हो (५)

11. *Man bāvarā bhayo*[27]

My mind has gone mad, o lord.

Fair one, stop prancing. Your lover
is in your own body.
The one he loves
is the true blessed bride.
Who cares
about dark or fair?
Stone by stone, people build
a palace and say, 'My house.'
Not my house! Not your house!
We're birds, just here for the night.
The traveller ties his bundle and camps
at an inn. Traveller, if there's someone to meet,
meet now! This is it!
A woman flings her hair and weeps:
my mate—our bond—broken.
Kabir says, listen seekers, friends,
the one who joined you
broke you.[28]

11. *Man bāvarā bhayo*

मन बावरा भयो मोरा रे स्वामी (टेक)
डगमग चाल छांड़ दे गोरी, घट में बसे पीय तेरा
जाको पिया चाहत सोही सुहागन, क्या गोरा क्या सांवरा (१)
कंकर चुन चुन महल उठाया, लोग कहे घर मेरा
ना घर मेरा ना घर तेरा, पंछी लीन बसेरा (२)
गांठ बांध के चला मुसाफिर कीन्ह सराया में डेरा
मिलना होय सो मिल ले मुसाफिर यहीं हमारा फेरा (३)
लट चिट कर तिरिया रोवे जोड़ा बिछुड़ गया मेरा
कहे कबीर सुनो भाई साधो जिन जोड़ा तिन तोड़ा (४)

12. *Māyā mahāṭhaganī ham jānī*[29]

Maya's the great swindler—now I know.
Trailing the noose of three qualities,
she wanders, whispering
honeyed words.

For Vishnu she's Lakshmi,
For Shiva she's Shakti,
for priests an idol,
for pilgrims a river.
For a monk she's a nun,[30]
for a king she's a queen,
in one house a jewel,
in one a shell.[31]
For a devotee, she's a pious lady,
For Brahma, Mrs Brahma.
Kabir says, seekers, listen well,
this is a story
no one can tell.

12. *Māyā mahāṭhaganī ham jānī*

माया महा ठगनी हम जानी
तिरगुण फास लिये कर डोले, बोले मधुरी बाणी (टेक)
केसव के कमला ह्वै बैठी, शिव के भवन भवानी
पंडा के मूरत ह्वै बैठी, तीरथ में भई पानी (१)
योगी के योगिन ह्वै बैठी, राजा के घर रानी
काहू के हीरा ह्वै बैठी, काहू के कोड़ी कानी (२)
भक्तन के भक्तिन ह्वै बैठी, ब्रह्मा के ब्रह्मानी
कहे कबीर सुनो भाई साधो, ये सब अकथ कहानी (३)

13. *Naiharvā ham kā na bhāvai*[32]

I don't feel right in my parents' place.

My lord has a city of perfect beauty
where no one comes or goes,
there's no moon or sun,
no water or wind.
Who will carry this message?
Who will tell the lord of my pain?
I can't see the path ahead,
and going back would be a shame.
Oh beloved, how can I reach
my in-laws' house?
Separation burns fiercely.
The juice of sensuality
keeps me dancing.
Without a true guru
no one is ours,
no one can show the way.
Kabir says, listen friends, seekers,
even in a dream my love won't come
to put out these flames.

13. *Naiharvā ham kā na bhāvai*

नैहरवा हम का न भावै
साईं की नगरी परम अति सुन्दर, जहँ कोई जाय न आवै (टेक)
चांद सूरज जहँ पवन न पानी, को संदेस पहुंचावै
दरद यह साईं को सुनावै (१)
आगे चलो पंथ नहीं सूझे, पीछे दोष लगावै
केहि विधि ससुरे जाऊँ मोरी सजनी, बिरहा जोर जरावै
विषैरस नाच नचावै (२)
बिन सतगुरू अपनो नहिं कोई जो यह राह बतावै
कहत कबीरा सुनो भाई साधो सुपने न पीतम आवै
तपन यह जिय की बुझावै (३)

14. *Naiyā morī nīke chālan lāgī*[33]

My little boat is sailing smoothly.
No storms or thunderclouds engulf it.
This seeker's very lucky!

I have no dread of capsizing,
no fear of the depths.
Turning upside-down won't even
muss my hair!
If a mountain should fall
in my boat,
I wouldn't feel the load.
I surrender
to the blessed teacher
who showed me the way.
Kabir says, someone who rows
without a head
can speak this truth.
A rare boatman knows the worth
of this untellable story.

14. *Naiyā morī nīke chālan lāgī*

नैया मोरी नीके नीके चालन लागी
आंधी मेघा कछु ना व्यापे, चढ़े सन्त बड़भागी (टेक)
उथले रहतो डर कछु नाहिं
नाहीं गहरे को संसा
उलट जाय तो बाल न बांका (१)
औसर लागे तो परवत बोझा
तऊँ न लागे रे भारी
धन सतगुरुजी ने राह बताई
ताकी रे मैं बलिहारी (२)
कहे कबीरा जो बिन सिर खेवै
सो यह सुमति बखाने
या बहु हित की अकथ कथा है
बिरला खेवट जाने रे (३)

15. *Nirbhay nirguṇ guṇ re gāūngā*[34]

Fearless, formless,
that's the form I'll sing, yes,
I'll sing, I'll sing!

I'll bind
the root lotus,
make the breath
flow upward.[35]

I'll make the mind
and feelings
still
the five elements
one.

Right, left, middle
channels—I'll bathe
where three streams meet.[36]

I'll catch the five
and twenty-five,
string them
on one thread.[37]

On the peak
of emptiness
where the unstruck sound
resounds, I'll sing
thirty-six ragas.[38]

Kabir says, listen,
truth-seekers,
I'll seize the sign
of victory.

15. *Nirbhay nirguṇ guṇ re gāūṅgā*

निरभय निरगुण गुण रे गाऊंगा (टेक)
मूल कमल दृढ़ आसन बांधू जी, उलटी पवन चढ़ाऊंगा (१)
मन ममता को थिर कर लाऊं जी, पांचों तत्व मिलाऊंगा (२)
इंगला पिंगला सुखमन नाड़ी जी, तिरवेणी पर न्हाऊंगा (३)
पांच पच्चीसो पकड़ मंगाऊं जी, एकहि डोर लगाऊंगा (४)
शून्य शिखर पर अनहद बाजे जी, राग छतीस सुनाऊंगा (५)
कहत कबीर सुनो भाई साधो, जीत निशान घुराऊंगा (६)

16. *Rām niranjan nyārā re*[39]

Unstained Ram is utterly other.
This spreading world is eye-shadow, brother.

Eye-shadow creation, the sound of Om,
eye-shadow vast expanse of space,
eye-shadow Brahma, Shiva, Indra,
eye-shadow Krishna with all his girlfriends.

eye-shadow poetry, eye-shadow Veda,
eye-shadow all your fine distinctions,
eye-shadow science, story, recitation,
eye-shadow all your useless information.

eye-shadow greenery, eye-shadow gods.
eye-shadow worshipers, eye-shadow rituals,
eye-shadow dancing, eye-shadow singing,
eye-shadow showing off all your categories.

eye-shadow—how far does it reach?
As far as austerity, pilgrimage, charity.
Kabir says, a rare one awakens,
dropping eye-shadow to touch
the unstained.

16. *Rām niranjan nyārā hai*

राम निरंजन न्यारा रे, अंजन सकल पसारा रे भाई (टेक)
अंजन उतपति ओ ओंकार, अंजन मांड्या सब बिस्तार
अंजन ब्रह्मा शंकर इंद, अंजन गोपीसंगी गोविंद रे भाइ (२)
अंजन वाणी अंजन वेद, अंजन किया नाना भेद
अंजन विद्या पाठ पुराण, अंजन फोकट कतहि गियान रे भाई (३)
अंजन पाती अंजन देव, अंजन की करे अंजन सेव
अंजन नाचे अंजन गावै, अंजन भेद अनंत दिखावे रे भाई (४)
अंजन कहौं कहां लग केता, दान पुनी तप तीरथ जेता
कहे कबीर कोई बिरला जागे, अंजन छाड़ि निरंजन लागे रे भाई (५)

17. *Ramaiyā kī dulhin luṭā hai bāzār*[40]

Ram's bride has looted the market.

She looted the cities of gods and snakes,
looted the three worlds, making a racket,
looted Brahma, Shiva, the great sage Narad,
put Shringi in his place, ripped Parashar's belly,
looted Kashi with a whisper long ago.[41]
After thinking about it, she looted
the lord of yogis.
I escaped by the lord's grace, got across
on the cord of the word.
Kabir says listen friends, seekers,
when that swindler comes,
stay awake.

17. *Ramaiyā kī dulhin luṭā hai bāzār*

रमैया की दुलहिन लूटा बाज़ार जी (टेक)
सुरपूर लूटा नागपूर लूटा तीन लोक मच हाहाकार
ब्रह्मा लूटे महादेव लूटे नारद मुनि के परी पिछार जी
श्रृंगी की मिंगी कर डाली, पारासर के उदर विदार
कन फूका चिर काशी लूटे, लूटे जोगेशर करत विचार जी
हम तो बचिगे साहेब दया से, शब्द डोर गहि उतरे पार
कहत कबीरा सुनो भाई साधो इस ठगनी से रहो हुसियार जी

18. *Sākhīya vā ghar sab se nyārā*[42]

Oh friend, that house
is utterly other
where he lives, my man,
my complete one.

There's no grief or joy,
no truth or lie,
no field of good and evil.
There's no moon or sun,
no day or night,
but brilliance
without light.

No wisdom, no meditation,
no recitation, no renunciation,
no Veda, Quran,
or sacred
song.
Action, possession, social
convention, all
gone.

There's no ground, no space,
no in, no out, nothing like
body or cosmos,
no five elements, no three qualities,
no lyrics, no couplets.[43]

No root, flower, seed, creeper.
Fruit shines
without a tree.
No inhale, exhale, upward, downward,
no way to count
breaths.

Where that one lives,
there's nothing.
Kabir says, I've got it!
If you catch my hint, you find
the same place—
no place.[44]

18. *Sākhīya vā ghar sab se nyārā*

सखिया वा घर सबसे न्यारा, जहं पूरण पुरूष हमारा (टेक)
जहं नहिं सुख दुख सांच झूठ नहीं, पाप न पुण्य पसारा
नहिं दिन रैन चंद नहिं सूरज, बिना जोति उजियारा (१)
नहिं तहं ज्ञान ध्यान नहिं जप तप, वेद कितेब न बानी
करनी धरनी रहनी गहनी, ये सब जहां हिरानी (२)
धर नहिं अधर न बाहर भीतर, पिंड ब्रह्मांड कछु नाहिं
पांच तत्त्व गुन तीन नहीं तहं, साखी शब्द न ताही (३)
मूल न फूल बेलि नही बीजा, बिना बृच्छ फल सोहे
ओहं सोहं अर्ध उर्ध नहीं, स्वासा लेखन कोहै (४)
जहां पुरूष तहवां कछु नाहीं, कहे कबीर हम जाना
हमरी सैन लखे जो कोई, पावै पद निरवाना (५)

19. *Satguru morī chūk sambhāro*[45]

My true teacher! Take care of me
in my endless failure.
I'm depending on you. My wit is poor.
Don't withdraw your blessed feet.

My cruel mind won't take advice,
I keep trying, but it defeats me.
All things happen through you, lord,
quickly take care.
Be with me now, true teacher,
redeem me. Let me forget
all other companions, let me love
only you. I've looked for help
everywhere in the world
and found nothing to rely on.
Kabir says, listen lord,
please take me across
the ocean of this world.[46]

19. *Satguru morī chūk sambhāro*

सतगुरू मोरी चूक संभारो
हौं आधीन हीन मति मोरी, चरनन ते जो ना टारो (टेक)
मन कठोर कछु कहा न माने, बहु वाको कहि मैं हारो (१)
तुमही ते सब होत गुसांई याको वेग संवारो (२)
अब दीजे संगत सतगुरु की जावे होय निसतारो (३)
और सकल संगी सब बिसरे, होऊ तुम एक पियारो (४)
कर देख्यो हित सारे जगत से मिल्यो न कोऊ पुनि सहारो (५)
कहे कबीर सुनो प्रभु मेरे भवसागर से हो तारो (६)

20. *Suntā hai guru gyānī*[47]

The guru, the wise one
listens. A voice vibrates
in the sky, subtle,
very subtle.

First something came
from energy-matter,[48]
then there was water.
Every body was totally filled
with the unseen, wordless
person.

Something came from there,
it was written down.[49]
Thirst quenched.
Giving up nectar,
running toward poison,
spreading the noose
upside-down.[50]

In the dome of the sky,
a cow gave birth.
Curds jelled on earth.
The saints ate butter, only butter,
normal people, poor things,
got whey.

Without ground, a circle appears.
Without a lake, water.
The dome of the sky
dissolves into light. The word speaks
from the guru's mouth.

An instrument plays
in-breath, out-breath

the three-point meeting place
shines with streams
right, left, centre
a banner
of emptiness
waves.

Kabir says listen friend, seeker,
this is the word beyond reach.
Eyes wide open all day
here's the sign:
no death, no decay.

20. *Suntā hai guru gyānī*

सुनता है गुरू ग्यानी ग्यानी ग्यानी
गगन में आवाज़ हो रही झीनी झीनी (टेक)
पहिले आये नाद बिंदु से, पीछे जमाया पानी
सब घट पूरण पूर रह्या है, अलख पुरूष निरबाणी हो जी (१)
वहां से आया पटा लिखाया, तृष्णा तो उने बुझाई
अमृत छोड़ सो विषय को धावे, उलटी फास फसानी हो जी (२)
गगन मंडल में गौ बियानी, भोई पे दई जमाया
माखन माखन संतों ने खाया, छाच जगत बपरानी हो जी (३)
बिन धरती एक मंडल दीसे, बिन सरोवर जूं पानी रे
गगन मंडल में होय उजियाला, बोले गुरूमुख बाणी हो जी (४)
ओहं सोहं बाजा बाजे, त्रिकुटी धाम सुहानी रे,
इडा पिंगला सुखमन नारी, सुन धजा फहरानी हो जी (५)
कहे कबीरा सुनो भाई साधो, जाई अगम की बाणी रे
दिन भर रे जो नज़र भर देखे, अजर अमर हो निशानी हो जी (६)

21. *Uḍ jāegā hans akelā*[51]

It will fly away alone, the swan.
What a sight: the carnival
of this world!

When a leaf falls from a tree,
it's hard for them to meet again.
Who knows where it will land
when it's hit by a gust of wind?

When your time is up,
the order comes down from above.
Death's mighty messengers arrive.
You have to tangle with Death.

Kabir sings the qualities of God
whose boundaries can't be found.
The guru moves on
according to his actions,
the disciple according to his.[52]

It will fly away alone, the swan.
What a sight: the carnival
of this world!

21. *Uḍ jāegā hans akelā*

उड़ जाएगा हंस अकेला, जग दर्शन का मेला (टेक)
जैसे पात गिरे तरुवर के, मिलना बहुत दुहेला
न जानू किधर गिरेगा, लग्या पवन का रेला (१)
जब होवे उमर पूरी, जब छूटेगा हुकुम हुज़ूरी
जम के दूत बड़े मज़बूत, जम से पड़ा झमेला (२)
दास कबीर हर के गुन गावे, वाहर को पार न पावे (३)
गुरू की करनी गुरू जाएगा, चेले की करनी चेला (४)

SONGS WITHOUT KABIR'S SIGNATURE LINE

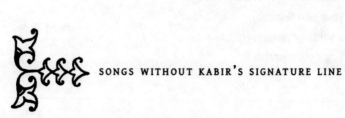

22. *Bholā man jāne amar merī kāyā—Gorakh*[53]

The childish mind is sure:
my body is immortal.
Wealth, youth,
fantasy of a dream,[54]
shadow of a cloud.

One well
five water-carriers
filling jars
with inconceivable liquid.

The well will cave in,
the bed will dry up,
the water-bearers will walk away
wringing their hands.

A stick of dry wood
gives no shade.
Where is your soul now?
Where are your fantasies?

Wall of sand,
pillar of wind.
Look in the shrine,
you'll get a surprise.

Machhinder, first among yogis,
your son Gorakh,
a solitary wanderer,
sings your praise.[55]

22. *Bholā man jāne amar merī kāyā—Gorakh*

भोला मन जाने, अमर मेरी काया
धन रे जोबन सपने सी माया, बादल की सी छाया (टेक)
एक कुवां पांच पनियारी, जल भरती है न्यारी न्यारी (१)
डट जायगा कुवा सूख जायगी क्यारी, हाथ मल मल चली पांचों पनियारी (२)
सूखा सा काट हेट नहि छाया, कहां तेरा हंसा कहां तेरी माया (३)
बालू की भीत पवन का खंबा, देवल देख भया है अचंबा (४)
आदि आदि नाथ मछंदर का पूता, ये जस गाय मेरा गोरख अवधूता (५)

23. *Gurā to jī ne gyān kī jaḍiyā daī—Shivguru*[56]

The guru has given
a root of wisdom,
the true guru has given
a root of wisdom.
That root is very dear to me,
filled with sweet nectar.

In the city of the body
is a big house.
In the middle of the house
is a secret.

Five male snakes,
twenty-five female snakes,
got a whiff of it
and fell down dead.[57]

A fierce goddess who ate[58]
the whole world
saw the true guru
and shook with fear.

Taking refuge in truth,
Shivguru says,
I crossed over
with my whole family.

23. *Gurā to jī ne gyān kī jaḍiyā daī—Shivguru*

गुरा तो जी ने ज्ञान की जड़िया दई, सतगुरूजी ने ज्ञान की जड़िया दई
वाही जड़ी तो म्हाने प्यारी जो लागे, अमरीत रस की भरी (टेक)
काया नगर में घर एक बंगला, जा बिच गुपत धरी (१)
पांचो नाग पच्चीसो नागनी सूंघत तुरत मरी (२)
आणि काली ने सब जग खाया, सतगुरु देख डरी (३)
सतवा शरणे शिव गुरु बोल्या, ले परवार तिरी (४)

24. *Gurujī jahāṅ baithūṅ vahāṅ chhāyā jī—Devanath*[59]

Oh guruji!
Wherever I sit, I find myself
in cool shade, and there
the lord
comes into view.[60]

As I sat among dense trees and plants
in the cool shade,
my true guru came and sat with me.[61]

My true guru ordered an earthen jar
from the potter
and raised
an offering.[62]

The body is the lock,
the word is the key,
my true guru opened it
and showed me.

In the city of the living being
the market is spread.
My true guru has provided
the goods.

Putting his two hands together,
Devanath says, a golden sign
marks my forehead.[63]

24. *Gurujī jahāṅ baithūṅ vahāṅ chhāyā jī—Devanath*

गुरूजी जहां बैठूं वहां छाया जी
सोही तो मालक (साहेब) म्हारी नज़रान आया (है) (टेक)
गेरा गेरा झाड़ झाड़ी शीतल छाया, म्हारा हो सतगुरू बैठन आया जी (१)
कुमारया जो घर से कलस्या मंगाया, म्हाने सतगुरूजी ने भेट चढ़ाया जी
(२)
तन भर ताला सबद भर कुंजी, म्हाने सतगुरुजी ने खोल बताया जी (३)
जीव नगर में हाट भराणो, म्हारा हो सतगुरुजी ने सौदे लाया जी (४)
दोई कर जोऊ देवानाथ बोल्या, म्हाणे केसर तिलक चढ़ाया जी (५)

25. *Gurujī maiṅ to ek niranjan dhyāūṅ jī—Gorakh*[64]

I meditate only on the one
the markless one
I don't keep company
with any other.

I have no sorrow, feel no pain,
call no doctor.
I've met the true teacher, the everlasting
healer. Only he
can feel my pulse.

I don't go to Ganga or Jamuna, don't bathe
in holy water. The sixty-eight holy places are here
in my body. Right here I wash away
every stain.

I don't tear off leaves, worship stones, visit temples,
don't chop wood in the forests,
don't torture any shrub.

Gorakh says, listen Machhinder,
I mingle light with light.
In the shelter
of the true teacher
coming and going
are gone.

25. *Gurujī maiṅ to ek niranjan dhyāūṅ jī—Gorakh*

गुरूजी मैं तो एक निरंजन ध्याऊं जी
दूजी के संग नहीं जाऊं जी (टेक)
दुख ना जानू जी, दरद ना जानू जी, मैं ना कोई बैद बुलाऊं जी
सतगुरु बैद मिले अविनाशी, वाको ही नाड़ी बताऊं जी (१)
गंगा न जाऊं जी जमुना न जाऊं जी, मैं ना कोई तीरथ न्हाऊं जी
अड़सठ तीरथ है घट भीतर, वाही में मल मल न्हाऊं जी (२)
पत्ती न तोड़ू जी पथर न पूजूं जी, ना कोई देवल जाऊं जी
बन बन की मैं लकड़ी न तोड़ू, ना कोई झाड़ सताऊं जी (३)
कहे गोरख जी सुनो हो मछिंदर, मैं ज्योत में ज्योत मिलाऊं जी
सतगुरु के मैं शरण गये से, आवागमन मिटाऊं जी (४)

26. *Gurujī mhāre mhāne dar lāgo vāhī din ro—Gorakh*[65]

Guruji, I'm afraid
of that day,
the day, the hour, the very moment.

In this body a garden blooming with flowers.
The deer is eating its way through the forest.[66]

In this body, a play of dust.
phuṭatā nī bāje ek raṇ ko.[67]

In this body a bustling market:
strike a bargain at this very moment.

In this body, Gorakh the ascetic says,
the day of bliss
is today!

26. *Gurujī mhāre mhāne dar lāgo vāhī din ro—Gorakh*

गुरूजी म्हारे म्हाने डर लागो वाही दिनरो
एक दिनरो (गुरजी) घड़ी आदि पलरो (टेक)
आणि तो काया में गरू फूला हंदी बाड़ी, मृग चरे राई बन रो (१)
आणि तो काया में गरू मट्टी के रमण का, फूटता नी बाजे एक रण को (२)
आणि तो काया में गरु हाट बज़ारा, सौदा कर ले घड़ि पलरो (३)
आणि तो काया में गरु जती गोरख बोले, आजरो दिन आनंद रो (४)

27. *Kāchī chhe kāyā thārī—Gorakh*[68]

Your body is an unbaked clay pot,[69]
it's false, a fantasy
o ram
all the writings you've written are false
o ram ram ram
Who made this raw body of yours
dear sir sir sir

In this pot is Ganga
o ram
in this pot is Jamuna
o ram
In this pot alone the holy bathing places
ram ram ram
In this pot is the lock
o ram
in this pot is the key
o ram
In this pot alone is the one who knows
how to open it
ram ram ram
In this pot is ripe mango
o ram
in this pot is green mango[70]
o ram
In this pot alone is the one who tastes them
ram ram ram
Through Machhinder's power
Gorakh the ascetic speaks.
One who understands this
is free.

27. Kāchī chhe kāyā thārī—Gorakh

काची छे काया थारी झुटड़ी छे माया राम,
झुटड़ा सलेख लिखाया राम राम राम
काची हो कोन घड़ेली थारी काया जी जी जी (टेक)
घट ही में गंगा राम घट ही में जमुना राम,
घट ही में तीरथ न्हाया राम राम राम (१)
घट ही में ताला राम घट ही मे कूंजी राम,
घट ही में खोलन हारा राम राम राम (२)
घट ही में अंबा राम, घट ही में अंबली राम,
घट ही में चाखनहारा राम राम राम (३)
मछिंदर प्रताप जती गोरख बोले
समझा सोई नर पाया (४)
घट ही में चाखनहारा राम राम राम (३)
मछिंदर प्रताप जती गोरख बोले
समझा सोई नर पाया (४)

28. *Lāgi hoy so jāne ho shabad kī—no signature*[71]

If you've been hit, then you know
the blow
of the word.
Find out what it's like to be hit, brother.
How else can you know the word?

In the street walks a wounded person
but you can't see the wound with your eyes.
An arrow shot from the bow of wisdom
has lodged in his heart.
It hit Anka and Banka, it hit that good butcher.
It hit Balakh Bakhar so hard
that he gave up his kingdom.
It hit Dhruv and Prahlad, it really hit Mira,
when it hit Gopichand, he put ashes on his head.

[The following stanza is in the Shilnath text and in folk versions. During research for this book, only one short recorded version by Kumarji was found, in a privately recorded form, lacking this closing stanza with Gorakh's signature line.]

Kill the five, control the twenty-five,
awaken the formless God,
Machhinder says, listen Gorakh:
Unfurl the flag of emptiness.

28. *Lāgi hoy so jāne ho shabad kī—no signature*

लागी होय सो जाने हो शबद की
लागी होय सो जाणिये म्हारा भाई, दूजा क्या कोई जाणे शबद की (टेक)
गेला मे एक घायल घूमे घाव नज़र नहीं आई
ग्यान कमठा पेर बैठा हिरदे मे भाल जमाई (१)
अंका लागी बंका लागी लागी सजन कसाई
बलख बुखार कू ऐसी लागी छोड़ चला बादशाही (२)
ध्रुव सो लागी प्रहलाद को लागी लागी हो मीरा बाई
गोपीचंद भरतरी ने लागी सिर में भस्मि रमाई (३)

[पांचाने मार पचीसन बसकर अनघड लेबोना जगाई,
कहे मछिंदर सुनो गोरख सुन में धजा फहराई (४)]

29. *Maiṅ jāgūṅ mhārā satguru jāge—no signature*[72]

I wake, my true guru wakes,
the rest of the world sleeps.

One is awake: a seeker in the jungle,
his consciousness fixed in the self.
One is awake: the king of the jungle,
his consciousness fixed on his kingdom.
One is awake: the mother of a child,
her consciousness fixed on the child.
One is awake: a deer in the jungle,
who searches ever, and never sleeps.[73]

29. *Maiṅ jāgūṅ mhārā satguru jāge—no signature*

मैं जागूं म्हारा सतगुरु जागे, आलम सारी सोवे (टेक)
एक तो जागे है जंगल का साधू, इसकी तो सुरत हम लावे (१)
एक तो जागे है जंगल का राजा, इसकी तो सुरत राजमाई (२)
एक तो जागे है बालक की माता, जिसकी सुरत बालक के माई (३)
एक तो जागे हैं जंगल का मिरगवा, भटक भटक जो निंद्रा खोई (४)

30. *Shūnya gaḍh shahar shahar ghar basti—Gorakh*[74]

In the empty fort, a city[75]
In the city, a settlement.
Who sleeps? Who wakes?
My love is mine, I am my love's.
The body sleeps, the spirit wakes.
In the empty fort, a city
In the city, a settlement.

Lotus in the water
buds among the lotuses
a bee smells the fragrance.[76]
This city has ten gates.
A yogi constantly
makes the rounds

Body a stone bowl,
mind a pestle,
he grinds with wisdom.
Five and twenty-five dwell in the body.
He pounds and gives them a drink.[77]

In the well of fire the adept practices,
practices, a master of heat.
Five disciples roam alone.
Unseen, Unseen,[78]
the mantra repeats.

A celestial woman steps forth,[79]
a second appears with made-up eyes,
a third beauty spreads the bed.
She's an unmarried virgin.

Before marriage she bears a son.
Mother and father rejoice.

Taking refuge in Machhinder,
Gorakh says, I meditate
on the indivisible one.

30. *Shūnya gaḍh shahar shahar ghar basti—Gorakh*

शून्य गढ़ शहर शहर घर बस्ती, कौन सूता कौन जागे है
लाल हमारे हम लालन के, तन सोता ब्रह्म जागे है (टेक)
जल बिच कमल कमल बिच कलिया, भंवर बास ना लेता है
इस नगरी के दस दरवाज़े, जोगी फेरी नित देता है (१)
तन की कुंडी मन का सोटा, ग्यान की रगड़ लगाता है
पांच पचीस बसे घट भीतर, उनकू घोट पिलाता है (२)
अगन कुंड से तपसी तापे, तपसी तपसा करता है
पांचो चेला फिरे अकेला, अलख अलख कर जपता है (३)
एक अप्सरा सामें उभी जी, दूजी सूरमा हो सारे है
तीसरी रंभा सेज बिछावे, परण्या नहीं कुंवारा है (४)
परण्या पहिले पुतुर जाया, मात पिता मन भाया है
शरण मछिंदर गोरख बोले, एक अखंडी ध्याया है (५)

NOTES TO THE SONGS

1 Text: Shilnath 198. Recording: *Avadhoota Bhajans* album. Malwi folksinger Bhairu Singh Chauhan has recorded a version of this song in a popular folk melody, on his cassette *Gurū binā koī kām na āve* (Without the Guru, No Success; Indore: Unix Music Co., 2004).

2 *Nirat surat ke bel banāvo. Nirat* and *surat*, often paired, refer to meditative states.

3 *Dubadhyā*, the first word in this line, coming just before *dūb* (grass), has stumped me and others I have consulted. I have taken a guess, associating *dubadhyā* with *duvidhā*, which means doubt or dilemma. This may be completely wrong, and I await further guidance. Tara Kini was reminded of a similar theme in a poem of Ramprasad, the famous Bengali devotee of Kali. She paraphrased Ramprasad's lines thus: 'You don't know the right way to do farming. If you put up a fence made from the name of Kali, then Jama (Death) can't come near. The seed is the name given by the guru. Water it with your devotion.'

4 The 'name' may refer to a name of God or to the Word or Sound that is the essence of all.

5 Text: Shilnath 234; *Nirguṇ bāṇī* programme. This poem is *shabda* 23 in the Kabir *Bījak* (Hess and Singh 2002: 49).

6 *Kudrat* is a Perso-Arabic word for nature, the divine power of creation. The line says nature's ways are *nyārī*—completely different (from what one might expect).

7 *Chhājnā*: to be fitting, suitable.

8 Text: Shilnath 59; *Saguṇ nirguṇ bāṇī* programme.

9 *Sabad anāhat*—'unstruck word'. One of the formulations used for the sound that the yogi hears within, a sound beyond subject and object, that emerges without the need for something that strikes and something that is struck.

10 'Simply' translates *sahaj*—simple, natural or spontaneous—and refers to the non-dual experience as well as to an informal 'school' in both Hinduism and Buddhism that speaks of ultimate reality as *sahaj*.

11 Text: *Madhyāntar* programme. Recording: *Rām Niranjan* album. This song is unusual in Kumarji's *nirguṇ* collection in that it uses a well-known animal tale of the sort found in the *Panchatantra* and *Hitopadesha*. The poet has adapted the moral tale to a *nirguṇ* message: we live in delusion about who we really are until a true teacher suddenly reveals to us our own nature. The musk deer is a common metaphor for the seeker who chases madly in search of a beautiful fragrance, not realizing it is located within herself. The final stanza brings us back to specifically yogic language, speaking of concentration between upbreath and downbreath.

12 I was able to listen to a private recording of this at the Komkali home in 2002. Kumarji laughed when he sang this line, and Vasundharji laughed when she heard it.

13 In the *Madhyāntar* programme we have *kar usavās*, which does not seem to mean anything. Tara Kini suggested it might be *karau savās*—dwells with. A version of this poem appears in Gangasharan Shastri, ed., *Mahābījak*, where the line says *karat soch pachatāt manahīman*: after reflecting in his mind, he regrets (his former delusion) (1998: 832).

14 *Ulaṭi āp meṅ āp samāna*: literally, 'the upside-down' (or reversed, turned-around) self enters into or merges with the self.

15 Text: Shilnath 166.

16 The cord—*ḍor* or *ḍorī*—is a recurring image in Kabir poetry of yogic practice. This subtle string is sometimes made of breath. It may be associated with *nām-jap*, recitation of the name, often with the help of a string of beads. The *ḍor* makes possible a connection—from lower to higher chakras, from a bound to a liberated state. Here the *hans*—swan, symbol of the pure, free spirit of a living being—rises on this cord to the heights (the *gagan manḍal*, the sky-circle, the thousand-petalled lotus at the crown of the head), the place of the *shūnya shikhar*, the peak of emptiness—*shikhar* suggesting a place at the top of the head as well as the top of a mountain.

17 The whole poem is in past tense, but the translation works better with present tense in the later lines.

18 *Nām*/name: one of several words Kabir uses for the essential sound or syllable. Kumarji apparently sang this bhajan rarely. Even the abundant private recordings that Mr Manohar received from Kumarji, and generously shared with me, do not include more than a one-minute presentation of this song's refrain (see Acknowledgements). By a wild case of serendipity, in 1992, I received the tape from Jeanne Fleming and Harlan Matthews described in the Preface. These four bhajans include two that no one except the family seems to have (the other being '*Ham pardesī panchchī bābā*'). I have not found any written version of '*Gurūjī ne diyo amar nām*', so this text is transcribed from listening. I have often heard the song in a folk version by P. S. Tipanya, the words of which make more sense to me in several places. For instance, Kumarji seems to say '*nām*' twice in the first line of the first stanza (*nām sarikha jo nām mat dijo ajān ne*), but that makes little sense. The folk version says *nām sarikha jo dān mat dijo ajān ne*. On my translation I have assumed the meaning of *dān* (gift) in the second position.

19 The Hindi line, according to the text Bhuvan Komkali showed me, is *ghughu dekhe tārā andhī/āndhī jyot*. It is unclear in the recording

whether the first vowel is long or short, thus whether the meaning would be 'blind' or 'storm'—both of which seem problematic to me. The folk version, which I have heard often, has *haṇḍī* in this position, which in Malwi is a connector with no substantial meaning. This makes more sense to me than either 'blind' or 'storm', so I have left the word untranslated.

20 Text: Shilnath 488.

21 Literally, 'all eight' *pahars*. The day is traditionally divided into eight parts/*pahars* of three hours each.

22 Text: Shilnath 14 and *Madhyāntar* programme. Recording: *Avadhoota Bhajans* album.

23 Five and 25: conventional numbers in Kabir poetry, standing for the five elements of nature and various combinations that amount to 25—all signifying our material existence. These numbers also appear in '*Gurā to jī ne gyān kī jaḍiyā daī*' (see p. 106). [See also NOTE 37.]

24 This song using the metaphor of weaving, showing the body as a fine cloth, is probably the most famous poem of Kabir. It is known virtually everywhere, sung by folk and classical musicians. Since Kabir was a weaver, it has an especially intimate connection with him.

25 Right, left, and centre are *ingalā*, *pingalā* and *sukhman*, the three major yogic energy channels in the body (also called, in more formal Hindi, *iḍā*, *pingalā* and *sushumnā*—see note 36).

26 In this, as in several other Kabir songs popular in Malwa, the marriage of a young girl is associated with death. The marriage bed becomes the stretcher on which a corpse is carried for cremation. Weddings are generally joyful occasions, yet fraught with conflicting emotions. The girl has to leave her family, often at a tender age, with a stranger-bridegroom, to live for the rest of her life with a family she doesn't yet know, in another village. The fear, grief and tears of this moment of parting are proverbial. The poet links this parting with the ultimate parting, conflating the eagerly anticipated bridegroom with death. The irony of the juxtaposition is dramatic: fertility turns to ashes; a rich new set of relationships turns to the ending of all relationships. The musical composition extends the

sense of irony. The tune is bright and lively, with Kumarji and Vasundharaji singing together and sounding quite happy even as the content becomes darker.

27 Text: Shilnath 159.

28 This stanza is almost identical to the closing verse of P. S. Tipanya's most popular Malwa bhajan, '*Zarā halke gāṛī hānko*' (Move your cart along gently), though the rest of the song is quite different.

29 Shilnath 257; *Nirguṇ bāṇī* programme.

Here, *māyā* with its great open vowels (like *nyārā* elsewhere) is the place Kumarji explores most extensively in his rendition. Unlike in the *nyārā* songs, there is something ominous in the sound of *māyā*, the first syllable slightly trembling, the second dropping down suddenly. Most remarkable is the way Kumarji's voice plays with *māyā*, drawing it out, making it quiver, giving it a loud flat sound, then a soft subtle one. I get the feeling that it is covering the whole of Creation, and that it is vaguely dangerous, powerful, shapeshifting. He also takes advantage of the vowel rhyme in the next two syallables, *māyā*. He explores the space of *māyā* many times, then suddenly utters *maya-maha*, and moves quickly to the revelation. The verb makes it seem that the speaker has just come to understand this:

> *Māyā mahāthaganī ham jānī*
>
> Maya is the great swindler, I have realized.

At the end of each stanza, we hear a repetition of the closing word, prosaic, like a thud of earthly reality. *Pānī. Kānī.*

Māyā, often translated as 'illusion', is a feminine personification of the ephemeral material universe, which is illusory in that it is constantly shifting, so that things are not what they seem. As it signifies the illusory power of phenomenal reality, it is a magnificent and potent concept in Indian thought. But for those of us interested in the construction of gender, it raises some problems. That the universe, this world, our bodies and faculties, are impermanent, constantly shifting, shimmering, confusing our perceptions, causing us to mistake illusion for reality, is not a problem. But that this power of illusion should be figured as a seductive woman, and that the victims of her stratagems should most commonly be represented as men—that is. In this song, *māyā* is not just a *ṭhag* (cheat, criminal) but explicitly a female *ṭhag*, a *ṭhaganī*. Most of the lines faithfully follow the pattern of a male figure misled by his female counterpart. But some lines take us beyond this—the holy water of a pilgrimage place, the idol of the pandit, the jewel or the shell kept carefully by its owner, are all gender-free, opening out the understanding of *māyā* to an ungendered space.

30 In the original, *yogī* and female *yogī* (*yogin*). I used monk and nun, which are not quite right, to keep the line short and dynamic.

31 *Koṛī*, cowry, a shell sometimes used as a low-value coin.

32 This poem uses the metaphor of a city or country that is completely different from our world of suffering, craving and separation. Other examples in this volume are '*Ham pardesī panchhī bābā* ' and '*Shunya gadh shahar*'. The image in '*Sakhiyā vā ghar sab se nyārā*' is that of a house rather than a city or country—with the same meaning. Here, a woman's voice speaks simply and sadly of not liking the place where she was born (*naihar* is natal home or village) and not knowing how to find her way to the home of her husband.

33 Text: Shilnath 85; *Nirguṇ bāṇī* programme.

Nīke: an old colloquial word, little used in modern Hindi, that means good, fine, nice, beautiful, true (and corresponding adverbs). In 2006, I had a chance to hear an old private recording of this for the first time. The tune struck me as strange, wandering wide, without strong boundaries. I associated this feeling with the open sea that is the prevailing image. In the refrain, the words *āndhī meghā* (storms, thunderclouds), went up and down, with many repeats, as waves would move a boat on a turbulent sea. Some words that ended with vowels at the ends of lines (*bhārī*, *bakhāne*, *sansā*) opened in a remarkable way and did not seem to close but, rather, to trail off into infinity. The ocean is usually a fearful image in Bhakti poetry: it is the *bhavsāgar*, ocean of existence, where most of us drown. Devotees pray to God to take them across to the other shore. In this unusual song, the ocean has been transformed; it takes on the quality of *nirguṇ* realization—boundless, easy, free of fear. It is still dynamic, deep, full of movement, unpredictable—but no longer threatening. All lovers of Kumarji's music will be deeply grateful to the Komkali family for providing a beautiful, high-quality recording of this bhajan for the CD that accompanies this book.

34 Text: Shilnath 79. Recording: *Avadhoota Bhajans* album.

35 The verse refers to a yogic posture in which the *mūl* (literally, 'root'), the lowest chakra or lotus, is 'bound' or closed. The breath is reversed (*ulṭī*), sent upward.

36 There are thousands of channels (*nāḍī*) in the body through which life-energy flows, but the three most important are called *iḍā*, *pingalā* and *sushumnā*. *Iḍā* and *pingalā*, on the right and left sides of the body (also called sun–moon, Ganga–Yamuna, etc.) represent the pairs of opposites, the in and out, coming and going movements that characterize normal ways of living and thinking. *Sushumnā* in the centre is the place where duality can disappear. Where the three meet is *triveṇī*—a term that has both inner and outer meaning for Indians, who know it as the place (in present-day Allahabad) where three holy rivers meet and where millions of pilgrims come to bathe at special calendrical moments.

37 Five, 25: five elements which combine with the five *prakṛitiyāṅ* (natural substances/processes) to produce 25 categories of physical experience. [See also NOTE 23.]

38 The term *shūnya*, emptiness, is prominent in yogic traditions and in Mahayana Buddhism. It signifies an experience of freedom and openness, a place where 'full' and 'empty' become synonymous. *Shikhar*, meaning peak or summit, is used both for a physical mountaintop and for the inner 'dome' within the head, where the experience of *shūnya* (also called *sahaj samādhi*, etc.) occurs as the reversed breath ascends to the highest *chakra*. The related word *shikhā* means a knot of hair at the top of the head. Yogic and *nirguṇ* traditions describe a sound that resounds (or roars) without one thing striking another. This sound doesn't belong to the world of duality.

Thirty-six is a conventional number that suggests all the ragas, all musical possibilities.

39 Recording: *Rām Niranjan* album.

A portion of the Introduction tells how Kumarji's melody and voice, combined with the rhymes and other sound effects of the words, challenge the translator. There is also the fact that *anjan* and *niranjan*, besides playing off each other in sound, have special cultural meanings that will not yield to English rendering without footnotes. So here is the note. *Anjan* means a black substance, literally 'lamp-black' / 'collyrium', used to mark something. It is most commonly a word for mascara or eye-shadow, used in India to outline the eyes of both women and children. For women, it is a beautifying cosmetic. *Niranjan* is *anjan* with a negative prefix. *Niranjan* might thus be understood as 'stainless' or 'markless'. It is also used to signify God in some *nirguṇ* sects. In this case, '*rām*' is linked with '*niranjan*' to emphasize that this is not the *saguṇ* Ram, the avatar of the Ramayaṇa story. Among the Nath Yogis and in the Niranjan Panth, Niranjan is a primary name of God.

Anjan's association with beautifying the body, and the way it plays with its contrary, *niranjan*, gives *anjan* a greatly expanded meaning in the song. It stands for all phenomenal existence, from the daily activities of human beings to the vast expanse of the universe. I have chosen to translate *anjan* as 'eye-shadow'. This has its drawbacks, but so do the alternatives, such as 'blemished', 'stained' or 'tainted'.

Another nice feature of the musical composition (besides those discussed in the Introduction): each four-line stanza has a repeating pattern for the first three lines, but in the fourth there's a sudden change. Extra syllables are squeezed into the line, the voice picks up speed to get them all in and it sounds more lighthearted, even humorous. A syncopation in the first line of each stanza also gives an unexpected bump to the listening experience.

40 Text: Shilnath 333.

41 *Kān phūkā chir kāshī lūṭe. Kān phūkā*, whispering in the ear, calls up the image of a religious initiation in which the guru whispers the mantra to the disciple. *Chir* could mean 'in the distant past' or 'rip / tear.'

42 Bhuvan showed me a family notebook in which *sakhiyā* was broken into what looked like two words, *sakhi + yā*. Since that makes no sense and appears to be an idiosyncrasy of handwriting, I have joined the word together here.

Kalapini explains that Kumarji sings this song in Bhairav, the 'ultimate raga for concluding a programme'. I am reminded of a conversation I had with P. S. Tipanya, the Kabir folksinger of Malwa, and his brother and co-singer Ashok, who sing this bhajan in a different tune. They said that this is one of those songs which has to be the last in a programme. After this, you can't say anything more.

I had a remarkable experience when Kalapini offered to play a private version of it for me one day in August 2003. Whatever I have heard and read about Kumarji's understanding of the special voice for singing *nirguṇ*, the way of 'throwing' the voice as discussed in the Introduction—for me, this version of *Sakhiya* will always represent that.

43 I took *shabda-sākhī* as referring to Kabir's two main verses forms: the lyric poem, called *shabda*, and the pithy couplet, or *sākhī*. *Shabda* literally means 'word' but is understood in *nirguṇ* tradition to refer to the unstruck sound that is heard in the experience of awakening. *Sākhī* literally means 'witness' and indicates that the verses express direct experience, not hearsay. Kalapini says Kumarji explained this phrase as 'no words to give witness'.

44 *Pāvai pad nirvānā*. The multiple meanings here defy translation. *Pad* = place; *pad* also means a song-poem like this one. *Nirvānā* is the Buddhist term for liberation, enlightenment, often used in *nirguṇ* and yogic literature. The negative prefix indicates something not happening. The Buddhist term is explained as blown out, extinguished. So *pāvai pad nirvānā* could mean 'you find the place of nirvana' (which is no place) or 'you find the song of nirvana' or 'you find nirvana in the song', or all of these. It could also be understood as *pad nir-bānī*, the place of no words.

45 Text: Shilnath 89.

46 This poem is quite untypical of the tone and style usually associated

with Kabir. In his signature line, Kabir most often addresses the human audience, almost never the lord. This supplication, with its unstinting declaration of failure and helplessness, has more the flavor of Tulsidas in the *Vinaya Patrika*.

47 Shilnath 263; also commonly sung by P. S. Tipanya and others in the Malwa folk tradition. I found a handwritten version in my friend Dinesh Sharma's old family collection of bhajan texts, kept at their village house and dating back about 100 years.

See discussion of this song in the Introduction. The verses evoke both Creation and its reversal—the latter being the yogic process of devolution, in which one returns to an elemental state, receding to origin, prior to complexity. Creating and uncreating become conscious processes in yoga; the emergence of the self reflects the creation of the universe, and the devolving back to uncreation is the meditator's process of dissolving the categories of mind and eventually the separate self. This process, parallel in micro- and macrocosm, is described in texts of tantric yoga. Certain terms in the song, like *nād* and *bindu*, are basic to tantric accounts of primal differentiation. See, for instance, Padoux (1990)

48 The line says: first it came from *nād-bindu*. What came? Perhaps that voice, the subtle voice that the *gurū gyānī* hears. The words *nād-bindu* refer to tantric representations of both the inner and outer universe, sometimes represented in a *yantra* or diagram with the *bindu* at the centre. *Bindu* is the centre, the drop, the seed of all matter; *nād* is sound, vibration. I have tried translating it as matter and energy. This is not bad, but it leaves out the associations of *nād-bindu* in Indian philosophy and practice.

49 *Paṭā likhāyā*. A *paṭṭā* is a title, deed, certificate, letter of authority. *Likhāyā* is causative form of 'to write': someone got it written. My guess is that this suggests the process of identity formation, reifying the self, making it official.

50 These lines are troublesome to me, as I have often heard them in another form that makes more sense to me. Kumarji's version says *tṛishna une bujhāī*, thirst was quenched. The folk version popular in

Malwa says *tṛishna nāhiṅ bujhānī*—thirst was not quenched, which casts an entirely different meaning on the lines that follow. The meaning in the folk verison works better in the context of Kabir's usual themes. It shows someone caught in delusion, unable to satisfy his thirst (*tṛishna*, the same word as in the second noble truth of Buddhism, craving, the cause of suffering). This person gives up divine nectar, runs toward poison—a common trope in Kabir—and gets caught in the snare of delusion (the same word, *phās*, is associated with *māyā* in '*Māyā mahāthaganī*', and elsewhere with *kāl*, death).

What does it mean to say, as Kumarji does, that thirst *was* quenched? Why would a person who was quenched, satisfied, free of delusion, give up nectar and rush toward poison? Kalapini gave a Shaiva interpretation, which she had heard from her father. These lines, she said, point to Shiva, who absorbed the poison that came out in the famous myth of the churning of the ocean. All the gods and anti-gods were waiting for the nectar of immortality to come out of the ocean. First various other things came out, including a terrible poison, which Shiva swallowed and kept in his throat. No other god could do that. Shiva alone can absorb this poison and extinguish our thirst. With this interpretation, the upside-down noose or snare refers to the rising of *kuṇḍaliṇī*.

The Shilnath collection gives the words exactly as Kumarji sings them. In the old handwritten version I found in Bagli village—a household manuscript dated 1928 but copied from an older collection belonging to the family of Dinesh Sharma—the line is negative: thirst was *not* quenched. When I told P. S. Tipanya of the Shaiva interpretation, he found it amusing and said Kabir had nothing to do with Shiva.

51 This is the unique text that was discovered by Kumarji embossed on a mirror in the Shilnath Dhuni Sansthan. I have not seen it in any other written source. The recording is available on the *Avadhoota Bhajans* album and can be heard online at www.musicindia online.com, under Kumar Gandharva, devotional.

52 It is hard to translate this succinct last verse, which comes across well in Hindi but not in English. *Gurū kī karanī gurū jāegā, chele kī karanī chelā*. It suggests that *karma*, our actions, shape our path, and we can't

blindly depend on the guru. The outcome for both guru and disciple will be shaped by their acts.

53 Text: Shilnath 105. Recording: *Jhīnī Chadariyā* album. It would be much more common in a phrase like this to say *bhūlā man—bhūlā* meaning lost, confused, deluded. The Shilnath text says *bhūlā*, but Kumarji distinctly says *bhola*, which means naive, innocent, childlike.

54 In this song, I'm made the unusual choice to translate *māyā* as 'fantasy'.

55 While Kabir typically addresses the listener in his signature line, Gorakh and other Nath poets addresses the guru. Traditionally Gorakh was the disciple of Matsyendranath (Machhinder in dialect). The last line, *ādī ādī nāth machchandar kā pūtā, ye jas gāy merā gorakh avadhūtā*, is not entirely clear to me, especially the word *merā*.

56 Text: *Saguṇ nirguṇ bāṇī* programme. Recording: *Rām Niranjan* album.

57 This stanza is not in the *Saguṇ nirguṇ bāṇī* printed programme but is in the sung versions, both by Kumar Gandharva and in the folk tradition. This is another instance of the 5–25 formula that we have seen several times before.

58 The line names Kali as the one who ate up the world. This seems to reflect how people who are not Kali worshippers might regard her as an emblem of a ferocious and frightening female energy. In recent years (possibly in response to questions from me and others), P. S. Tipanya has begun to insert *māyā* in this line to clarify the meaning—so in his version of the song he often says *inī kālī ne māyā sab jag khāyā . . .*

59 Text: not found in Shilnath or in any printed programme. Recording: *Ram Niranjan* album. It is quite challenging even to transcribe. Special thanks for help from Tara Kini and Surajit Bose.

60 I am understanding the feminine pronoun *mhārī* as referring to *nazarān*, the common Hindi form, *nazar*, being feminine. Shade and coolness are very positive symbols in Indian poetry, in contrast to the burning hot sun (which is associated with the heat of desire). However, in other contexts, the sun has a different and positive

meaning, associated with the brilliant light of awakening (as in English: illumination, enlightenment).

61 Kumarji seems to pronounce the first word without aspiration, as *geḍā* or *gerā*; my consultants and I have not found a meaning for such a word. We could take it as *gheṛā*, surrounded (by trees), or as *gaharā*, deep or dense. I have taken the latter meaning.

62 The jar is *kalasyā*, not the more common *ghaṭ*. A *kalash* is the sort of jar often used in ritual. The 'offering' sustains the ritual context, but the jar must still represent the body. Is the guru's offering the gift of the body itself? Is it the *shabda*, the word, mentioned in the next verse?

63 Who is placing the golden mark on whose forehead? Who is making an offering to whom? I have found no agreement on these questions.

64 Text: *Gīt varsha* programme.

65 Text: Shilnath 198. Recording: *Avadhoota Bhajans* album.

In several stanzas, Kumarji throws in the phrase *he bhāī* or *are bhāī*, (oh brother!) typical of Malwi folk style. There are several unsolved translation problems in the poem.

66 In the line *mṛig chare rāī ban ro*, I don't know how to translate *rai*.

67 I am stumped by this line and haven't heard any satisfying explanations. Let us hope for a future edition where this and other mysteries will become clear.

68 Text: Shilnath 143.

69 The raw, or unbaked, clay pot is a common image for the body. Here we get 'unbaked body' (*kāchī kāyā*) in the refrain, and 'clay pot' (*ghaṭ*) in the stanzas.

70 Tara Kini told me that *ambla* and *amblī*, which had perplexed me, can mean ripe and green mango.

71 Text: Shilnath 151.

72 Text: Shilnath 332. See Kumar Gandharva's reference to this song in the Introduction.

73 This suggests the proverbial musk deer, driven to find the source of a beautiful fragrance. Enlightenment comes at the moment when the deer realizes the fragrance is within itself.

74 Text: Shilnath 131; *Madhyāntar* programme.

75 The word for fort here is *gaḍh*. To the ear it can easily sound like *ghar*, house. P. S. Tipanya sings it as *ghar*, and in the second phrase Kumarji says *ghar*.

76 I have taken this as *bhaṃvar bāsan letā hai*, the bee smells the fragrance, though it could also be *bhaṃvar vās na letā hai*, the bee doesn't settle / dwell anywhere, or *bhaṃvar vāsanā leta hai*, the bee feels passion.

77 Who is grinding and who is drinking is obscure to me. *Soṭā* and *kunḍī*, translated here as bowl (as in mortar) and pestle, have also been explained in quite different ways. A *kunḍī* can be a staff or club, a *soṭā* a doorchain or bolt. Kalapini suggested that *kunḍī* here could be a key.

78 *Alakh* (unseen) is a mantra and an exclamation associated with Nath yogis. The supreme being is often called *Alakh Niranjan*.

79 The *apsaras*, a beautiful, female, supernatural being, appears often in Puranic stories, usually to tempt a meditating sage and thereby break his concentration. There is a story that Gorakh's guru, Macchinder, got caught in illusion, was tempted by a beautiful woman, married and had children. Gorakh came and rescued him. Short versions of this story were told to me by Kalapini Komkali and by a gentleman named Vyas in Dewas.

Avsān / PASSING AWAY

An Essay by Ashok Vajpeyi

Truly to sing takes another kind of breath.
A breath in the void. A shudder in God. A wind.[1]
Rainer Maria Rilke

What to say about death—it's not our world.
Kumar Gandharva

In the middle of the sky-circle, that enlightened guru certainly heard his voice.[2] But we, here on this dusty earth, enmeshed in the business of our lives, have been listening to his voice for years. Despite disease and old age, he kept bringing forth that song of flourishing trees, spreading vines.[3] Sitting on Shiva's platform he sang, and, as Madhu Limaye had said years before on his 60th birthday, 'It seemed to us that we were touching the mystery of this world.' This time he had a premonition of his end. A week earlier, without any warning, he turned up in Indore to meet his friends. He had been telling his wife and daughter that the distress this time was beyond anything he had experienced. This time I won't stay. Every time, I marshal all my forces to fight. Then something new comes along.

He even spoke of the direction in which he wished his dead body to lie. He had said that his last rites should be in the same place as everyone else's, not any special place. He had asked his tabla accompanist to go to the cremation ground and see how it felt. He added that the place shouldn't feel bad. A person going there should feel, 'I have come to a nice place.' When the funeral procession, after passing through the streets of Dewas with full state honours, reached the public cremation ground, surrounded by lush green fields, it really did feel like a park. Many intimate friends of Kumarji were there, along with the public from Dewas and Bhopal, many artists from Bhopal, Indore, Ujjain, Dewas and so on. The fire was lit by his son, the singer Mukul Shivputra, who had arrived from a temple in Nemavar just in time for the funeral procession. In that cremation ground encircled by green grasses, the pyre burned. But whose passing away was it? Kumar Gandharva's, or Shivputra Siddharamaiya Komkali's?

Kumar Gandharva had made his wager with death and sustained himself with untiring courage for nearly half a century. He had spent most of his musical life singing with only one lung. With his irrepressible will to live, he had held death back for almost 50 years. For him, singing became synonymous with living. The will to live and the will to create could not be separated. More: for him, to live was not merely to be alive but to live questioning and inquiring, meeting every unexpected and unpredictable turn of events with courage and dignity. Kumar Gandharva considered himself a practitioner of the most perishable art. 'Every day I die singing,' he said. We are all perishable in the same way, even though, in the entanglements and perplexities of our lives, we tend to forget it. Kumarji always remembered his mortality; he was an artist who was assaulted not by death but by the fullness of life, its innumerable sensations. Since his initial illness had brought him very close to death, in a sense he always remained close to it without falling victim to it. His music is a daring counter-image, without any self-pity, for this perishing condition.

Throughout his life, with ebullient curiosity, Kumar Gandharva seemed to be searching for the life-giving meaning of this inescapable mortality. His music had an astounding fearlessness. Such a vast canvas of emotion that it contained everything: truly another kind of 'breath', 'void', 'shudder', 'wind'; a boundless, never-ending artistic passion. From passionate desire to carefree nonchalance to imperturbable detachment—all this in the music of one musician. There are great singers who are incontrovertible masters of a particular style or artistic emotion. But Kumar Gandharva sang everything with equal command and involvement—*khayāl, thumrī, tarānā,* bhajan, *ṭappa.* He could bring forth countless artistic emotions with equal depth. He was the supreme singer of *nirguṇ*, yet he was also a powerful exponent of the *saguṇ* presence of words and poetry. In his singing, from beginning to end, he sustained a kind of peaceful tension. Everything flowed, emotion-charged, in that singing: passion and dispassion, joy and grief, nature exquisite and restless, solitude and community, awesome power and impenetrable silence, loquaciousness and calm, duality and oneness. Musical imagination had rarely bestowed such experience, such abundance and fullness of rich feeling, on any one musician.

In demolishing the myth of *gharānā* membership, Kumar Gandharva radically redefined our tradition and our times. Not by repetition and duplication, but by experimentation, he brought forth the creative ambiguity of traditional truth. To experiment and find something new, he emphasized, we don't need to go outside of tradition but to grapple with it and delve deep into it. He was not ready to believe that repetition, shunned in other artistic media, was desirable in music, the art of all arts. He was one of the very few musicians who believed, and participated in, a far-reaching community of artists. He took a deep interest in poetry, painting, theatre, architecture. Although, following custom, he had had little schooling, he was a great reader. In his house, 'Bhanukul', he had a collection of about 2,000 books, which he kept in careful order and read constantly. When you met him, he would ask—have you read this prose-piece by Vinda Karandikar, or such-and-such a book by Iravati Karve?

It was no coincidence that he attempted to make music a matter of reflection and dialogue. Raga, composition, beat, tempo, emotional expression—he was a constant, alert, eager questioner of all. This questioning showed itself both within and beyond music. Conservatives shied away from such abundant questioning. They had no answer to the question of why Kumarji, while he had all the musical notes and skills at hand, still produced ragas in such strange and unexpected forms. Dhrupad singer Ramakant Gundecha said that after setting forth all the notes of Yaman, Kumarji would go searching for Raga Yaman. It is not that he lacked respect, but that he refused to see thinking and questioning as destroying or opposing that respect.

Just as he put an end to the conservative hostility between tradition and experimentation, he also startlingly reduced the distance between classical and folk. Apart from him, no musician has ever had the temerity to present a two-and-a-half-hour performance consisting only of folk music, as he did in his 'Malwa Folk Melodies' concert. For the first time in the twentieth century, and the last, the stability of classical and the dynamism of folk, the dignity of classical and the energy of folk, found a graceful balance. He placed classical consciousness in the stream of folk culture, recognized the aristocratic in a refined version of the ordinary. From the folk to the classical, he brought passion, fragrance, the sense of touch. With regard to everything—whether god, saint, the given world, any structure or pattern of the status quo—he spontaneously raised his finger, questioning. Perhaps no other musician has posed such a continuous challenge to the classical status quo and, in his particular way, left behind the indelible stamp of his thought and perception. In a sense, Kumar Gandharva throughout his life was the 'opposition' in classical music. His music was in many ways a counter-music. At the same time, he was alert to the danger of being turned into an establishment himself. He had no desire to start his own tradition, but insisted on keeping his thought independent.

Kumar Gandharva changed at one go the foundation of prevailing musical aesthetics. In making change central to music, he made it entirely modern. Though he may not have written a conventional essay on classical music, whenever he expressed his ideas, and most of all whenever he assimilated those ideas in his music, he created by example a new aesthetic that only needs to be gathered together in order to be understood.

Kumar Gandharva gave words and poetry a new prestige in classical music. It is widely agreed that his singing deepened our understanding of Kabir, Sur, Mira and so on. But it is important to remember that, in doing so, he did not devalue the sovereignty of the voice (*sur*). Words had their place, even their greatness; but the medium of meaning in music is the voice. On this he always insisted, in both thought and action.

Kumarji, with his genius for waging battles, viewed opposition to the status quo as a necessary duty, and he fought on several fronts at once. He composed new *bandish*es under the pseudonym 'Shok' [sorrow]; he created new ragas; he collected in writing lost compositions of Kabir, Gorakhnath and others. He did this without ostentation or theatricality. If he created a new raga, he placed it before music-lovers for their enjoyment and reflection, with humility; he did not call a press conference and make a proclamation.

In his ordinary conversation, poetic expressions came forth effortlessly. He was at once the Kabir (who burns his own house) of Indian music and the *rasik-grihasth* (connoisseur householder) of its tradition. While he was intellectual and often argumentative, his singing had an irrepressible sensuality. In the growing disconnection of this age, he was at once the poet of affection and the passionate architect of a vast detachment. His first book, *Anūp Rāgvilās* (Bombay: Marg Prakashan, 1965), was published long ago. He had been thinking for several years about publishing a new book called *Saguṇ Nirguṇ*. He creatively brought forth the wholeness of that pair, *saguṇ* and *nirguṇ*. Through him a new taste developed for classical music—not only among many young people, but also among poets, writers, painters, dancers, architects and so on. He played a decisive role in bringing the classical together with the modern, on his own terms.

There is a certain fear that Kumar Gandharva's passing away might mean the passing away of renewal, restless questioning, new ideas in classical music. These anxieties may be postponed for a while. As long as the qualities of courage, imagination and originality remain possible, along with contemporaneity and dynamism within the classical, Kumar Gandharva will remain with us as a true messenger and a vigilant watchman. The iconoclastic tradition has written one more indelible name on time and on our collective memory—Kumar Gandharva.

Notes

This essay has been reproduced from Vajpeyi (1999: 72–6).

1 My Berkeley friend, Rilke translator Anita Barrows, kindly provided me with the German lines and reference for this epigraph, so that I would not get lost trying to translate a Hindi version of the German. It is from the third Sonnet to Orpheus. The original German:

In Wahrheit singen, ist ein andrer Hauch.
Ein Hauch am nichts. Ein Wehn im Gott. Ein Wind.

The English translation is from Barrows and Macy (2005).

2 Vajpeyi refers to the bhajan '*Suntā hai gurū gyānī*'; see text and translation (bhajan no. 20) as well as discussion in the Introduction.

3 Vajpeyi (1999) writes that Kumarji still sings of '*drum drum latā latā*', literally, 'tree-tree, vine-vine', the repetition signalling a profusion of these green and growing things. These are words from one of the *bandishes* that Kumarji sang.

ACKNOWLEDGEMENTS

It's strange to have acknowledgements at the end of a book, but I'm a devotee of a poet who often sends his message upside-down.

A long time has passed since my last book was published, so I have a lot to acknowledge. In the Preface I have highlighted my gratitude to those people who have truly made this book possible: the Komkali family in Dewas, Ashok Vajpeyi and U. R. Ananthamurthy. Here, I would like to continue my song of wonderment at the way the networks of learning, support, collaboration, struggle, laughter and love spread through the universe like Kabir's smooth, knobbly, coloured, shiny, dirty, subtle, opaque, translucent warp and weft—boundless but embodied.

It is our extraordinary good fortune that this book's cover is graced by a painting by Gulammohammed Sheikh, one of India's greatest living artists. In 1999 he exhibited a group of paintings called *Kahat Kabir*, 'Kabir

Says'. In the years that followed, images of Kabir continued to appear in his art. It is worth quoting some of his comments from a 2001 interview:

> I have admired Kabir since my schooldays . . . . His life and words represent pluralities. There was no one religion, or one system of belief or one idea, but multiple systems, multiple religions and multiple ideas. I think in the 15th–16th centuries, there was also not the separation we have today of the secular and the sacred. The sacred had a place in the secular, and vice versa. And sacred was not just something that was housed in a temple or a mosque: singing could be an act of worship, painting could be an act of worship. . . .
>
> Over the years Kabir kept returning to me in many ways, often through music. When Kumar Gandharva sings Kabir the words become molten. Time and again I heard Kumarji's bhajans, and I began to think: if he can sing Kabir, can I not also paint him? I have wanted to paint Kabir for a long time, but it is only in the last two years that I felt able to paint him. In painting him, I have engaged with the image of Kabir—based on the popular, conventional icon and also a wonderful late Mughal image that I came across. But I have equally, or even more, been engaged with the relationship between my images and his words, the relationship that can exist between painting and writing. . . . There is a very meaningful relationship between writing and painting. . . . Our painting tradition has been suffused with it. But now we have developed a purist mode in which we have isolated the two. This is like saying that while you see you should shut your ears, while you hear you should you're your eyes. You don't, you can't! Those who have studied the processes of perception tell us that in the mind when a word is thought, an image is instantly perceived, and when an image is perceived, it is instantly named in our minds (Sheikh 2001).

For seven years I have gone back and forth to a little village in Malwa, Madhya Pradesh, drawn there by a singer of Kabir to whom I was introduced in 2000 by Ashok Vajpeyi and Kapil Tivari, Director of the Adivasi Lok Ḳala Parishad in Bhopal. Prahlad Singh Tipanya and his family in Lunyakhedi village have given me a rural home in India, a spiritual home of devotion to Kabir and a musical home of vibrant, beautiful folk melodies, voices, instruments, travels and performances. This opened the world of oral Kabir to me; it opened me to receive oral Kabir and to feel the vital interconnections of words and music. This experience continually informed and supported my efforts to enter the depths of Kumar Gandharva's Kabir.

Prahladji's wife Shanti, their children Ajay, Vijay and Sona, their grandchildren, Prahladji's brothers Ambaram and Ashok, their wives and children, the old patriarch of the family Daji, along with the cows, buffaloes, mud, green landscapes, often malfunctioning jeeps—all these come forth in the imagination when I think of how I learned about Kabir in Malwa. To other Kabir singers, like Narayan Singh Delmia and Kaluram Bamaniya, and accompanying musicians like Ajay, Ashok, Devnarayan and Manoj, I also offer heartfelt thanks.

Anu Gupta and Arvind Sardana are my best friends in Dewas. Who can tell how many chais and 10 a.m. lunches this means, how many nights sleeping in their living room and (after the house expansion) in the fine bedroom upstairs, how many conversations about work and life (often talking over the soap operas and film songs Bali was watching on TV), how many kilos of dahi and paneer from the dairy near Motibangla Chauraha? What does all this have to do with Kabir? Kabir knows!

Anu and Arvind work for the highly respected educational NGO Eklavya, which did groundbreaking work with Kabir singers through most of the 1990s. In sharing that work with me, they—along with other workers of Eklavya from that period, like R. N. Syag and C. N. Subramaniam—opened up endless vistas in understanding oral Kabir and the living Kabir traditions of Malwa.

Dinesh Sharma, a key organizer of Eklavya's Kabir project, and Suresh Patel, who has independently carried it forward in new forms in Indore, have provided great help and inspiration.

The Soni family of Dewas have been amazingly warm and generous friends. Kailash and Garima have provided a haven, nourishment and shared love of Kumar Gandharva's music. Their eldest son Ambuj has been an unfailing source of practical help whenever I asked, and often when I did not.

Krishna Kant Shukla, a singer who is deeply devoted to Kumar Gandharva and his music, joined me for part of my travels, shared his stories and knowledge, was the first to tell me about the *Shīlnāth Śhabdāmṛit* and let me make a copy of that important book as well as copies of the Kumar Gandharva concert programmes he had collected over the years.

Purushottam Agrawal, former Professor of Hindi literature at Jawaharlal Nehru University, current member of the Union Public Service Commission, and extraordinary scholar and writer about Kabir, has shared his knowledge and original insights on Kabir for years. It is always a special pleasure to meet with him and his wife, Suman, in Delhi.

Gay Searcy has been a deeply valued counsellor and companion during the years that this book was in progress.

Tara Kini of Bangalore, brilliant teacher and teacher of teachers, Hindustani classical singer, Kumar Gandharva-lover, fabulous swimmer, mischievous and unpredictable chum famous for her startling gift of colour-coordination in clothing, constant consultant who kept helping me refine translations and solve conundrums in Kumarji's bhajan texts up to the last moment—how can I thank her? By promising that we'll dance together on the bed whenever, on whatever continent, we may meet.

Tara introduced me to Mr M. S. Manohar, an architect of Mumbai who was such a deep admirer of Kumarji's music that the singer gave instructions that he should regularly be given copies of concert recordings. In the same spirit of generosity, Mr Manohar has shared copies of those precious recordings with people who had good reason to want them. In September 2007, he gave me three MP3 discs with dozens of songs (many of which I had never had the opportunity to hear), along with a neatly typed catalogue of everything. I bow in gratitude to Mr Manohar and his gracious family.

Can I possibly say what I owe to Shabnam Virmani? Yes—I owe her nothing. She taught me about true friendship, free giving and receiving. For six years (and counting), she has been my constant companion in our 'Journeys with Kabir'—the title she had given to her remarkable series of films, CDs and books. Shabnam, her husband Arvind Lodaya, and their son Sahir, have opened their home to me for months at a time, an arrangement we laughingly called the Heritage Writer in Residence programme. This book was mostly written at their home in the Heritage Apartment complex, Yelahanka, Bangalore. Beyond Heritage, we travelled everywhere you can imagine, from rural India to upstate New York, from Pondicherry to Vancouver to Stanford, drenched in Kabir music and thought, hotly pursuing the meanings of yogic terminology and Malwi linguistic oddities, hanging out with Prahladji, consulting endlessly on her films and my books and articles, singing and singing. She has given fine-grained comments on multiple drafts of this book, as I have done on her films. Her set of four feature-length documentary films, together with other audio, video and written productions, were released in 2008 (see www.kabirproject.org). This paragraph can only hint at what we have shared. Heartfelt gratitude also to Arvind, Sahir, Mary.

Though merely reading Kabir didn't do it, moving in the worlds of Kabir music and living traditions has helped me understand the meaning and value of the guru, the true teacher, wherever he or she might turn up. With awe I remember the high-school teachers who nurtured me as a person, writer, and poetry lover. Eckoe Ahern read aloud to us in tenth grade (with an unforgettable voice for Eeyore the morose donkey) and at graduation inscribed tenderly in my yearbook not 'Write to me' but 'Write *for* me.' She is long gone from this world, but vivid in my memory. Recently departed from this world is my hero George Gross, who modelled passion for poetry (Keats!) and gave me, you might say, everything. As my English teacher for several years, he opened the doors of great literature, serious thought, even humorous grammar. He and his late wife Marlo loved me and saved my life more than a couple of times. *Mhārā satguru baniyā bhediyā, mhārī nāṛī re pakaṛī haṅ.* 'My true guru was a revealer of secrets, he grasped my wrist and felt my pulse.'

The friends and teachers, bells and cushions, bowls of food and cups of tea at Berkeley Zen Center are a source of life, love and awakening. *Hoshiyār rahanā re, nagar meṅ chor āvega. Jāgrat rahanā re, nagar meṅ jam āvegā.* 'Stay alert, a thief has entered the city. Stay awake, death has entered the city.'

The American Institute of Indian Studies has been a lifeline in my research and writing for over 30 years, during which I have benefited from five AIIS fellowships. Their short-term grant in 1999–2000 allowed me to scout and sketch out the project on Kabir oral traditions, and the senior fellowship in 2002 allowed me to do it. Everything I have ever published on matters Indian is directly indebted to AIIS and to its people, including Pradeep Mahendiratta, Purnima Mehta, all the staff in Delhi, and Elise Auerbach in Chicago.

My family—Kaz and our two grown-up kids, Karuna and Ko—have inspired me with their creativity and steadfast unconventionality. Karuna, maker of stories, scripts and films, actor, my partner in swimming and hot-tub sitting, remarkably focused and determined, wise and sensitive. Ko, passionately devoted to his garden, committed to undermining capitalism and the culture of greed, connoisseur of found t-shirts and third-hand boots, calm companion, kind man, ever wittier than I. Kaz, wild painter, supplier of sushi, prolific author, who jogs in the basement and in his spare time works to create a world without armies. Kabir didn't praise family life, but I do.

Richard Schechner bumped into me in Varanasi in 1976 and nudged me in the direction of thinking and writing about performance. This resonated with my own desire to let literature jump up off the page and reveal itself as living in people's minds, hearts, bodies and communities. The first publication that resulted from Richard's nudging was an article we co-authored on the Ramlila of Ramnagar in 1978. The latest is this book. In September 2006, we met in Varanasi again. Having breakfast on the veranda of the Ganges View Hotel, we discussed our current projects. 'Do you have anything we can put in our Enactments series?' he asked, speaking of the series he and Carol Martin were co-editing for Seagull Books. 'Well, there's this little book on Kumar Gandharva and Kabir.' 'Let's do it,' said Richard after a short discussion, and then he introduced me to Naveen Kishore, beginning the process that would lead to publication with this superb and groundbreaking publishing house. My thanks to the team at Seagull Books, and to Richard, who, throughout these years of our friendship, has been generous, patient, visionary and fun.

BARROWS, Anita and Joanna Macy (trans and eds). 2005. *In Praise of Mortality: Selections from Rainer Marie Rilke's Duino Elegies and Sonnets to Orpheus*. New York: Riverhead Books.

BRIGGS, George Weston. 1973 [1938]. *Gorakhnāth and the Kānphaṭa Yogis*. Delhi: Motilal Banarsidass.

CALLEWAERT, Winand, Swapna Sharma and Dieter Taillieu (eds). 2000. *The Millennium Kabīr Vāṇī*. New Delhi: Manohar Publications and Sahitya Akademi (English introduction, Hindi text).

CHATTERJEE, Gautam. 2006. 'Finding the Goal Within'. *The Hindu, Friday Review Delhi* (14 April). Available at: https://bit.ly/3rK7F6I

DHARWADKER, Vinay. 2003. *The Weaver's Songs*. New Delhi & New York: Penguin Books.

GOLD, Daniel and Ann Grodzins Gold. 1984. 'The Fate of the Householder Nath', in *History of Religions*, 24(2): 113–32.

HESS, Linda. 1987. 'Kabir's Rough Rhetoric', in Karine Schomer and W. H. McLeod (eds), *The Sants: Studies in a Devotional Tradition of India*. Berkeley: Religious Studies Series, and Delhi: Motilal Banarsidass.

——. 'Three Kabir Collections: A Comparative Study', in Karine Schomer and W. H. McLeod (eds), *The Sants: Studies in a Devotional Tradition of India*. Berkeley: Religious Studies Series, and Delhi: Motilal Banarsidass, 1987.

——, with Shukdeo Singh. 2002 [1983]. *The Bijak of Kabir* (Trans. L. Hess and S. Singh; essays and notes by L. Hess). New York: Oxford University Press.

MENON, Raghava R. 2001. *The Musical Journey of Kumar Gandharva*. New Dehi: Vision Books.

MULLER-ORTEGA, and Paul Eduardo. 1989. *The Triadic Heart of Shiva*. Albany, NY: State University of New York Press.

PADOUX, Andre. 1990. *Vāc: The Concept of the Word in Selected Hindu Tantras*. Albany: State University of New York Press.

SHEIKH,Gulammohamed. 2001. *Palimpsest: Paintings 1998–2001*. Delhi: Vadehra Art Gallery.

SRINGY, R. K., with Prem Lata Sharma (trans). 1999. *Sangītaratnākara of Śārngadeva*. Delhi: Munshiram Manoharlal.

TAGORE, Rabindranath (trans.) (with the assistance of Evelyn Underhill). 1915. *Songs of Kabir*. New York, The Macmillan Company.

VAUDEVILLE, Charlotte. 1993. *A Weaver Named Kabir*. Delhi & New York: Oxford University Press.

WHITE, David Gordon. 1996. *The Alchemical Body: Siddha Traditions in Medieval India*. Chicago: University of Chicago Press.

HINDI

AGRAWAL, Purushottam. 2000. *Vicār kā anant*. New Delhi: Rajkamal Prakashan.

——. 2004. *Nij brahma vicār: dharma, samāj aur dharmetar adhyātma*. New Delhi: Rajkamal Prakashan.

—— (ed.). 2007. *Kabīr: sākhī aur sabd*. New Delhi: National Book Trust.

CALLEWAERT, Winand, Swapna Sharma and Dieter Taillieu (eds). 2000. *The Millennium Kabīr Vāṇī* (English introduction, Hindi text). New Delhi: Manohar Publications and Sahitya Akademi.

DVIVEDI, Hazariprasad. 1961 [1942]. *Kabīr*. New Delhi: Rajkamal Prakashan.

DVIVEDI, Kedaranath. 1965. *Kabīr aur Kabīr-panth, tulanātmak adhyayan*. [Kabir and the Kabir Panth, A Comparative Study]. Prayag/Allahabad: Hindi Sahitya Sammelan.

KOHLAPURE, Pandharinath. 2004. *Gānayogī Kumār Gandharva* (Kumar Gandharva, Yogi of Song; trans. from Marathi by Harshadray Dholakiya). Pune: Rajhans Prakashan.

SHASTRI, Gangasharan (ed.). 1998. *Mahābījak* [The Greater Bijak]. Varanasi: Kabir Vani Prakashan Kendra.

SHILNATH (ed.). 1923. *Ṣrī Shīlnāth Śhabdāmṛit* [The Nectar of Poetry: Shri Shilnath's Collection]. Dewas: Shri Shilnath Sansthan.

SINGH, Shukdeo (ed.). 1972. *Kabīr Bījak* [The Bijak of Kabir]. Allahabad: Nilabh Prakashan.

VAJPEYI, Ashok. 1999. *Bahuri akelā: kumār gandharva par kavitāen aur nibandh* [Among Many, Alone: Poems and Essays on Kumar Gandharva]. New Delhi: Vani Prakashan.

AUDIO RECORDINGS

It is unclear how many of Kumar Gandharva's recordings of Kabir and other *nirguṇ* bhajans are presently available in the market. All of his original commercial recordings came out as records (78 or LP) or cassettes. Some were later made into CDs. The information here is as complete as I can manage at present. A valuable discography of Kumar Gandharva has been compiled by Rajeev Patke at the National University of Singapore, and is available at courses.nus.edu.sg/course/ellpatke/Miscellany/kumar.htm. K. R. Tembe has also published a discography of Kumar Gandharva in *The Record News: Journal of the Society of Indian Record Collectors* 1 (January 1991): 22–6.

This page lists recordings going back to 1936 and provides links to excerpts from recordings of 1940 and 1958.

The major records and cassettes for Kumarji's *nirguṇ* bhajans are the following:

GANDHARVA, Kumar and Vasundhara Komkali. 1972. *Bhajan-Triveni.* Calcutta: Gramophone Company of India.

Includes: '*Nirbhay nirguṇ*'; '*Kaun thagavā*'; '*Avadhūtā yugan yugan ham yogī*'.

GANDHARVA, Kumar. 1982. *Pandit Kumar Gandharva Sings Nirguni Bhajans.* Calcutta: The Indian Record Mfg. Company Ltd.

Includes: '*Jhīnī Jhīnī bīnī chadaryiyā*'; '*Avadhūtā kudrat kī gat nyārī*'; '*Suntā hai gurū gyānī*'; '*Bholā man jāne amar merī kāyā*'.

GANDHARVA, Kumar. 1988. *Nirgun ke gun.* Calcutta: HMV India.

Includes: '*Hirnā samajh būjh*'; '*Uḍ jāegā hans akelā*'; '*Gurā to jine gyān kī jaḍiyā daī*'; '*Avadhūtā gagan ghaṭā gaharānī*'.

One more cassette was published by a company which subsequently disappeared. It seems to have included '*Rām niranjan nyārā hai*' and possibly '*Gurujī jahāṅ baithūṅ*'; '*Naiharvā*'; '*Māyā mahāṭhaganī*'; '*Sakhiyā vā ghar sab se nyārā* and '*Bin satguru nar rahta bhulānā*'. These have not been available in the market for some time, and I have not been able to trace the original cassette.

A 1958 HMV record includes a very early recording of the Kabir bhajan '*Jāg piyā re*', which I discovered late and therefore did not include in this book's collection. '*Naiyā morī nīke chālan lāgī*' is listed in Patke's discography as having been included in a 1969 recording from HMV.

CDs that have been made from the above sources include *Nirguṇ ke guṇ*, published by HMV (date unknown); *Avadhoota Bhajans* (EMI India, date unknown) and *Nirguni Bhajans* (Dunya, 2003). Various bhajans are available online as MP3 downloads, or can be heard / seen on YouTube.

The albums referred to as '*Rām niranjan*' and '*Jhīnī chadaryiyā*' (after the first bhajans on the copies) have disappeared from the market. I got a copy of a copy and no production details are available.

FILMS

PATEL, Jabbar (dir.). 2006. *Hans Akela: Kumar Gandharva*. Mumbai: Films Division of India, 90 mins.

VIRMANI, Shabnam (dir.). 2008. *Journeys with Kabir*: (i) *Had-Anhad / Bounded-Boundless: Journeys with Ram and Kabir* (103 mins); (ii) *Koi Sunta Hai* / Someone is Listening: *Journeys with Kumar and Kabir* (96 mins); (iii) *Chalo Hamara Des* / Come to My Country: *Journeys with Kabir and Friends* (97 mins); (iv) *Kabira Khada Bazaar Mein* / In the Market Stands Kabir: *Journeys with Sacred and Secular Kabir* (94 mins). Bengaluru: Srishti School of Art, Design and Technology. (For further information, please visit: www.kabirproject. org)

Kumar Gandharva: 1942–1992 Memorial Album. 2004. Dewas, Madhya Pradesh: Kumar Gandharva Sangeet Academy. Two DVDs: 64 mins and 86 mins, respectively. Not for sale.

INTERVIEWS

VIRMANI, Shabnam. 2004a. Interview with Shraddha Kirkire, Indore.

——. 2004b. Interview with Vinay Hardikar, Pune.

——. 2004c. Interview with Krishna Nath, Rishi Valley School, Madanapalle, Chitoor District, Andhra Pradesh.

——. 2004d. Interview with Neela Kirkire, Pune.